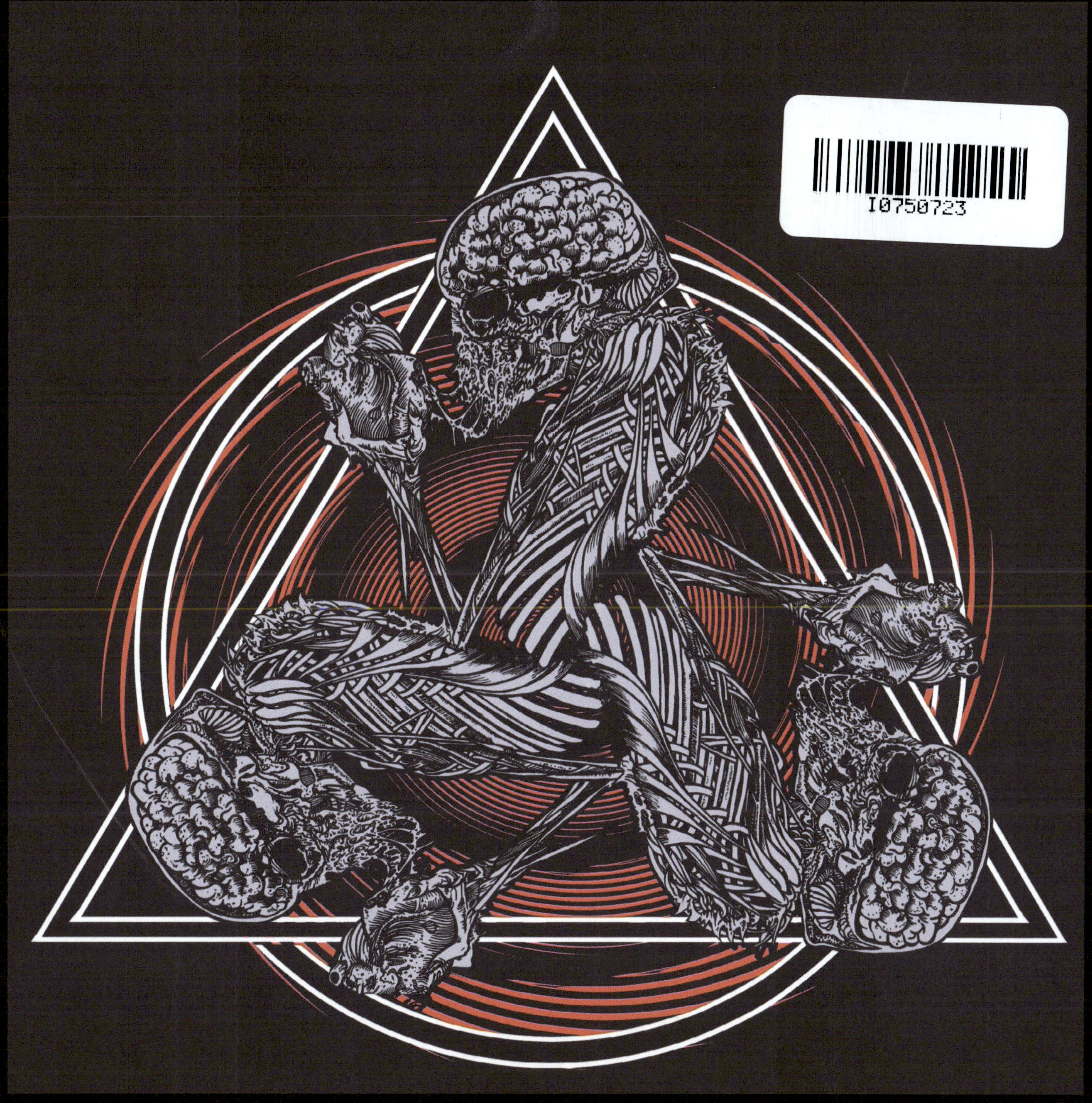

Illustration and design

by THOMAs AMBROsE DENNEY

www.tomdenney.com

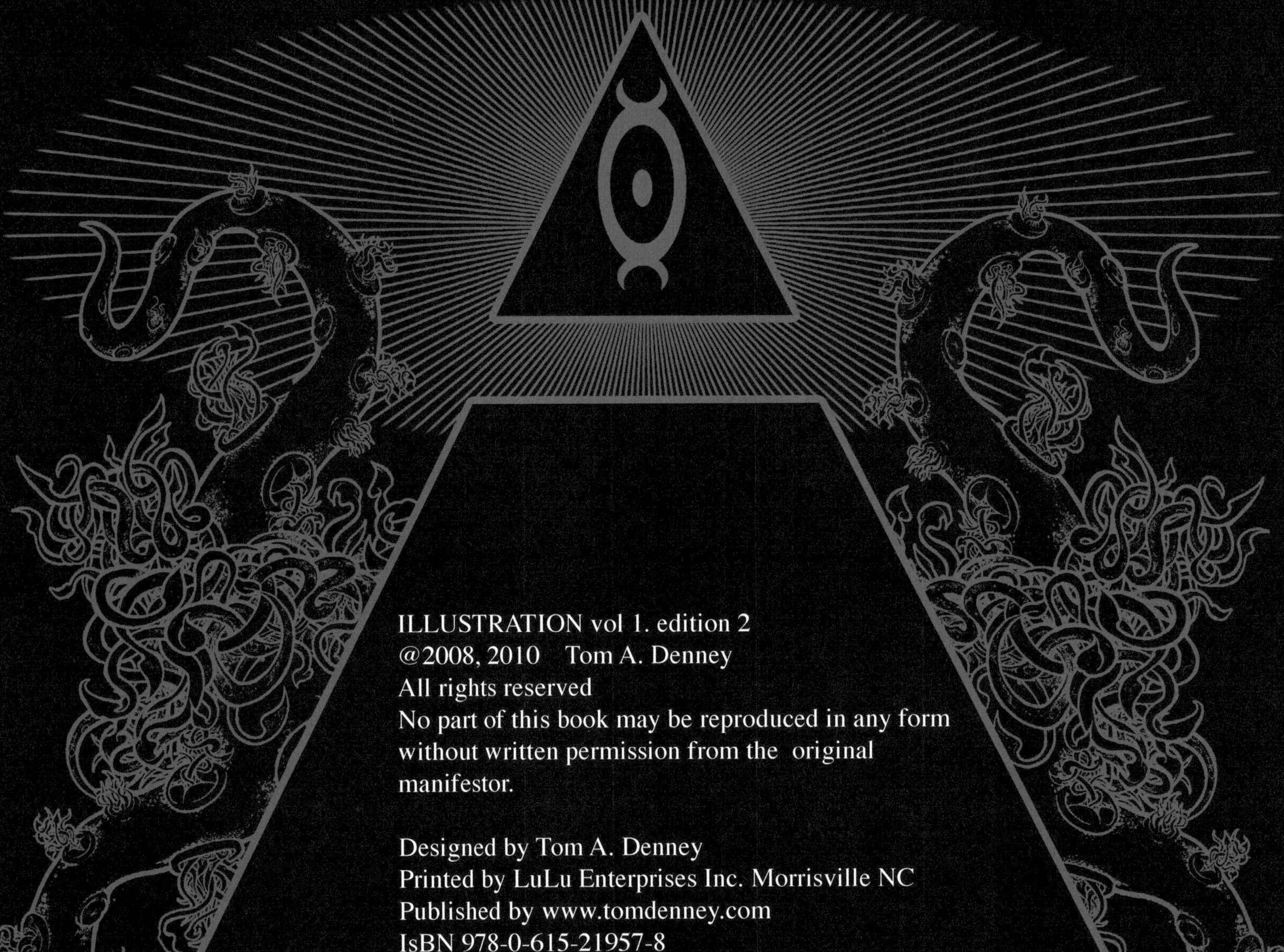

ILLUSTRATION vol 1. edition 2

Designed by Tom A. Denney
Printed by LuLu Enterprises Inc. Morrisville NC
Published by www.tomdenney.com
IsBN 978-0-615-21957-8
cover: Embracing the Circle

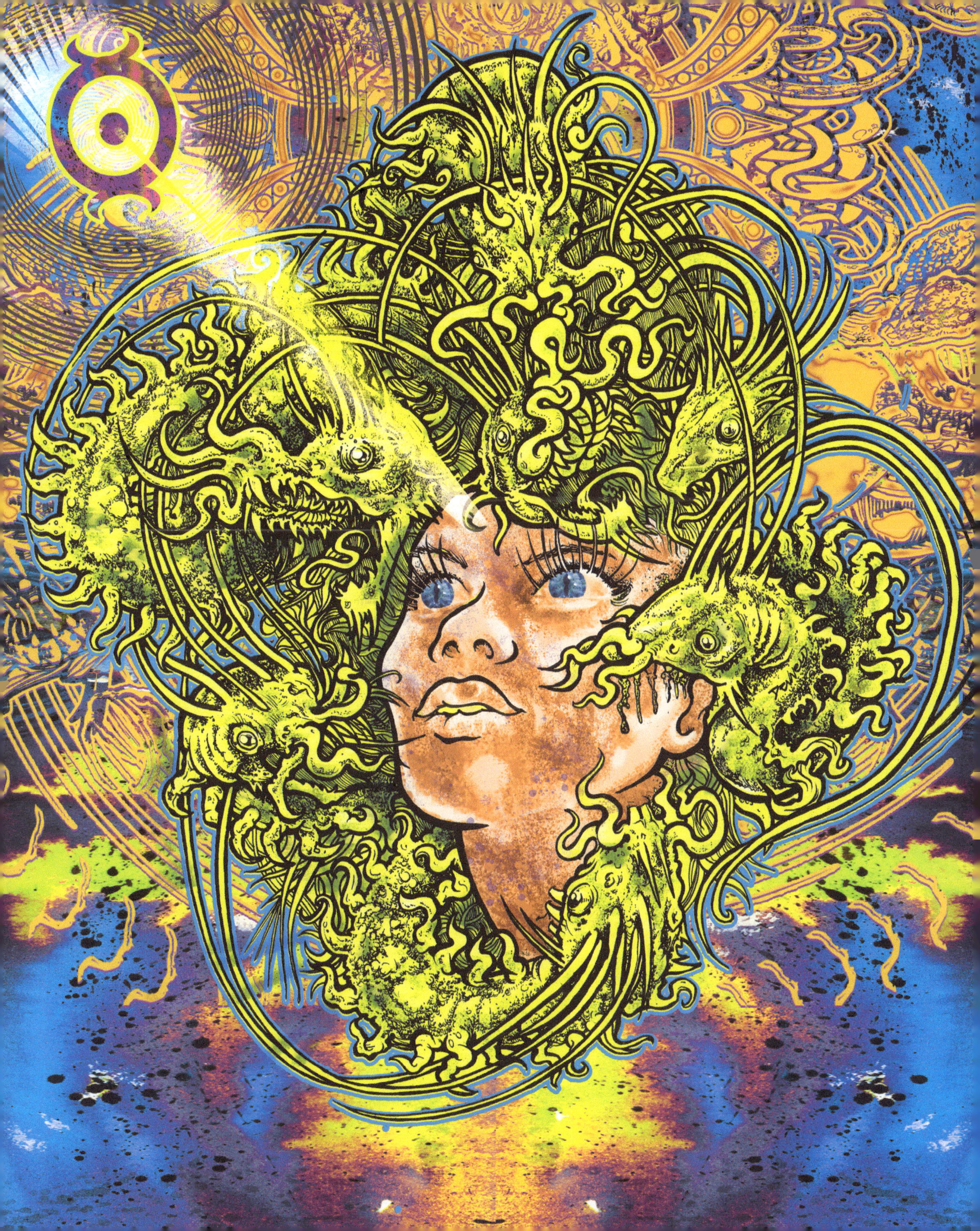

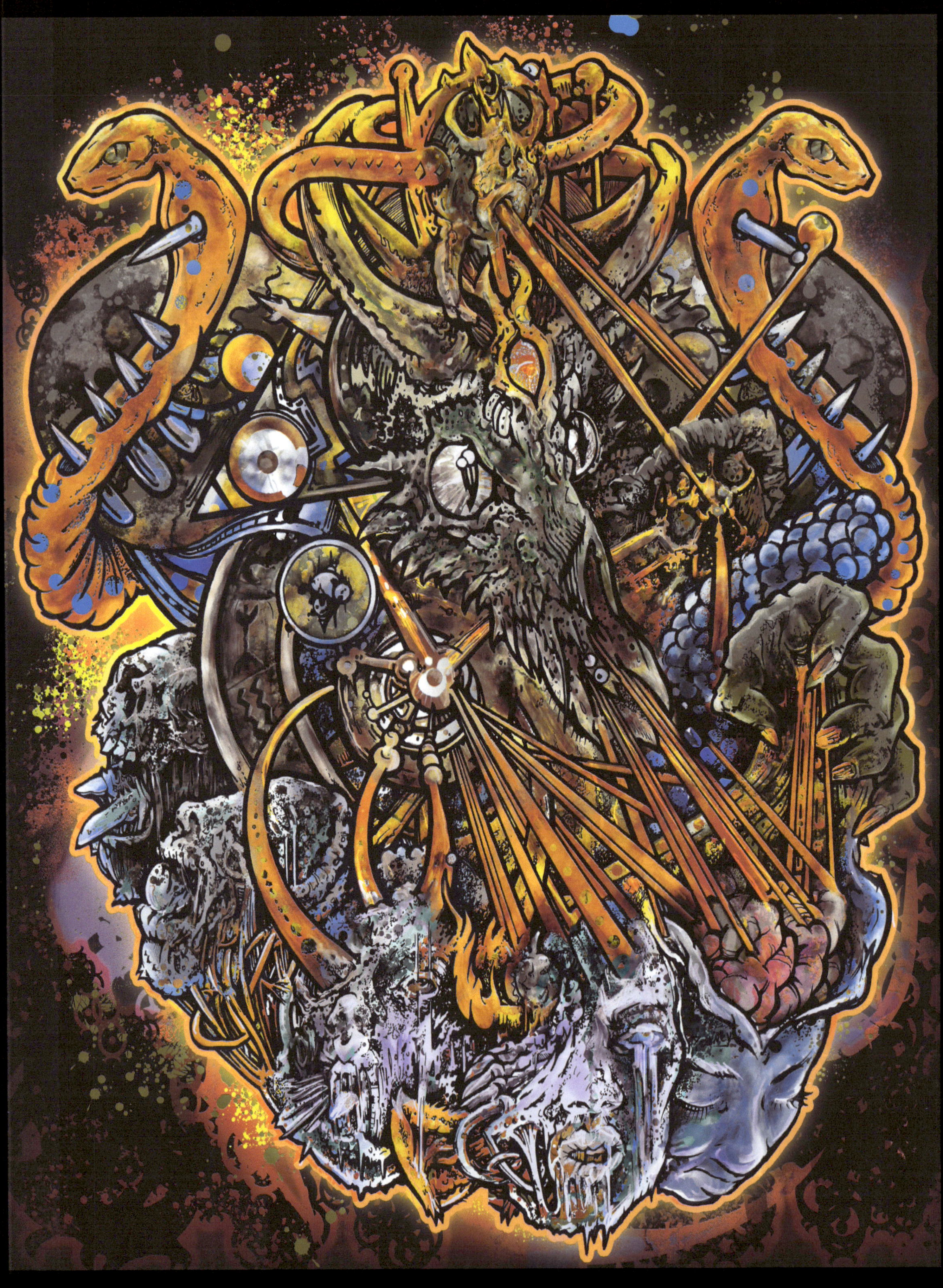

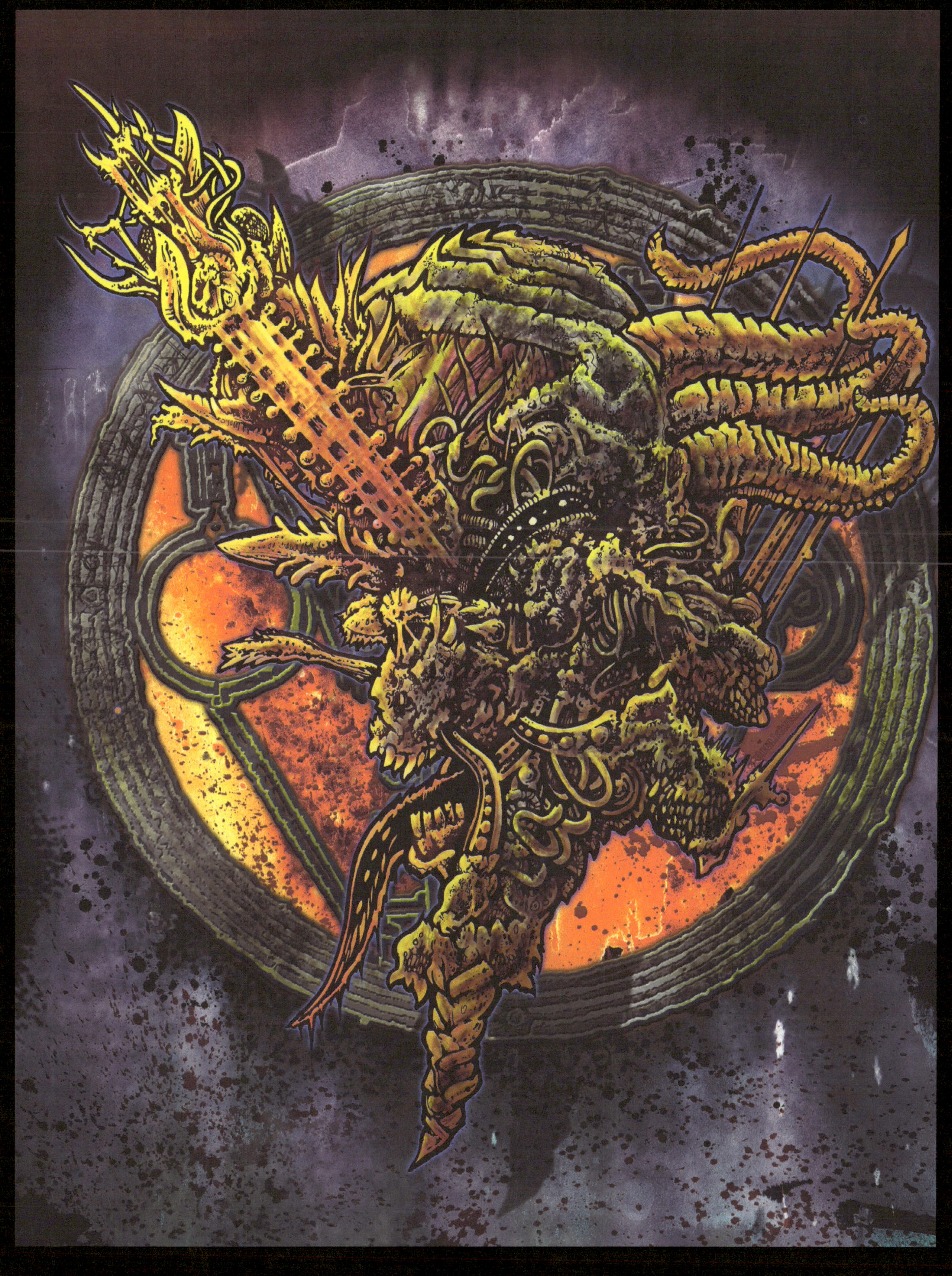

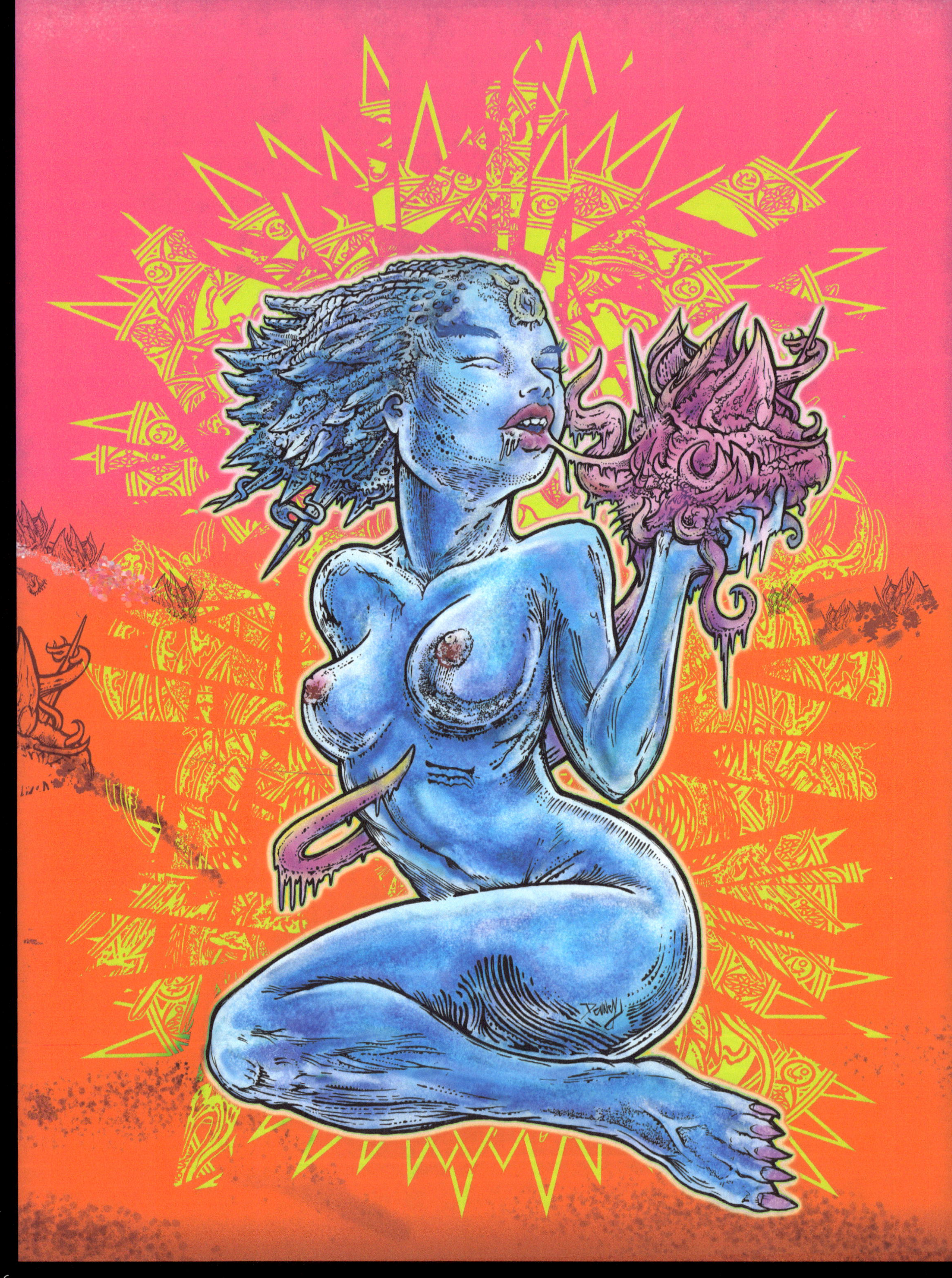

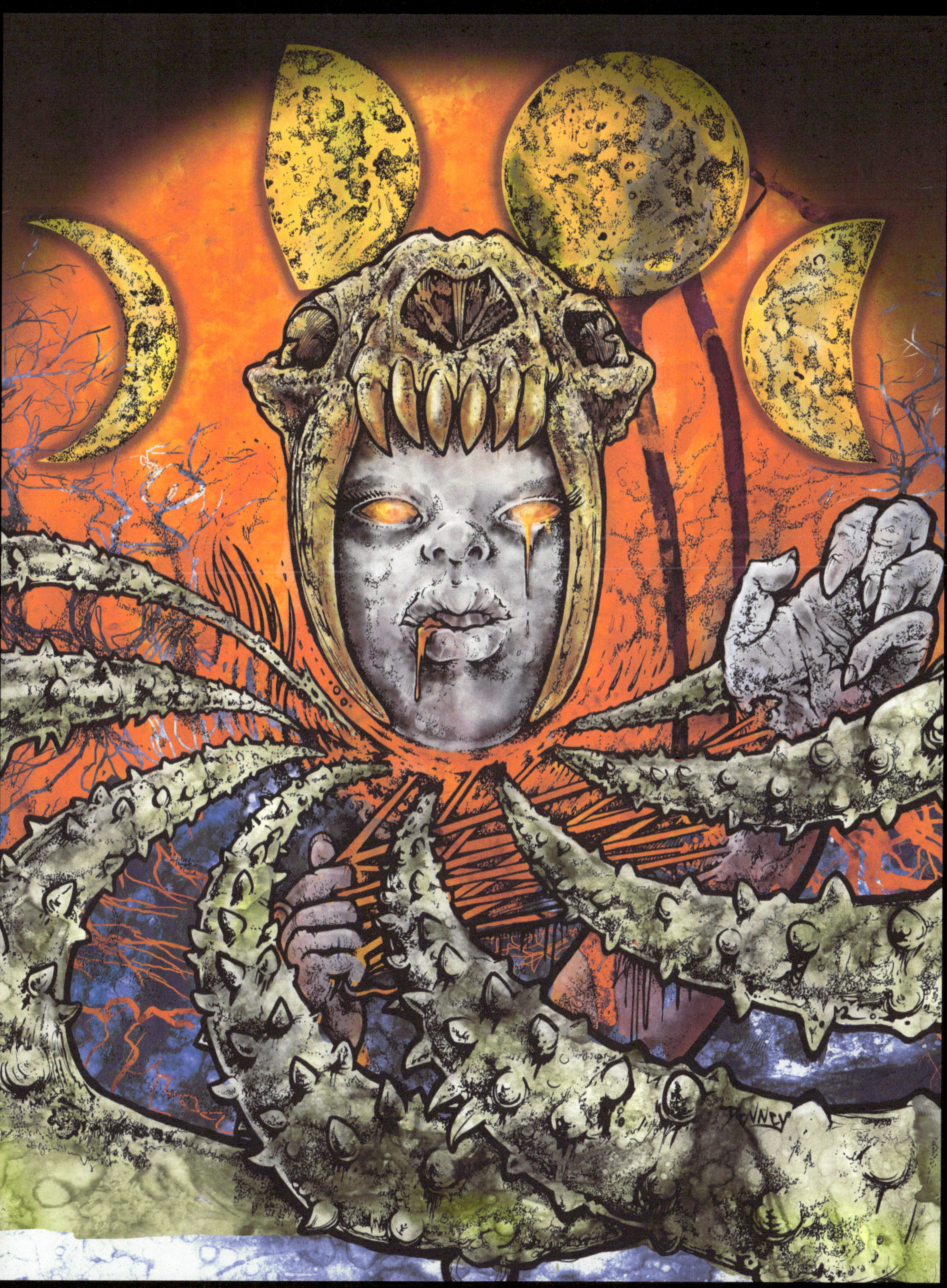

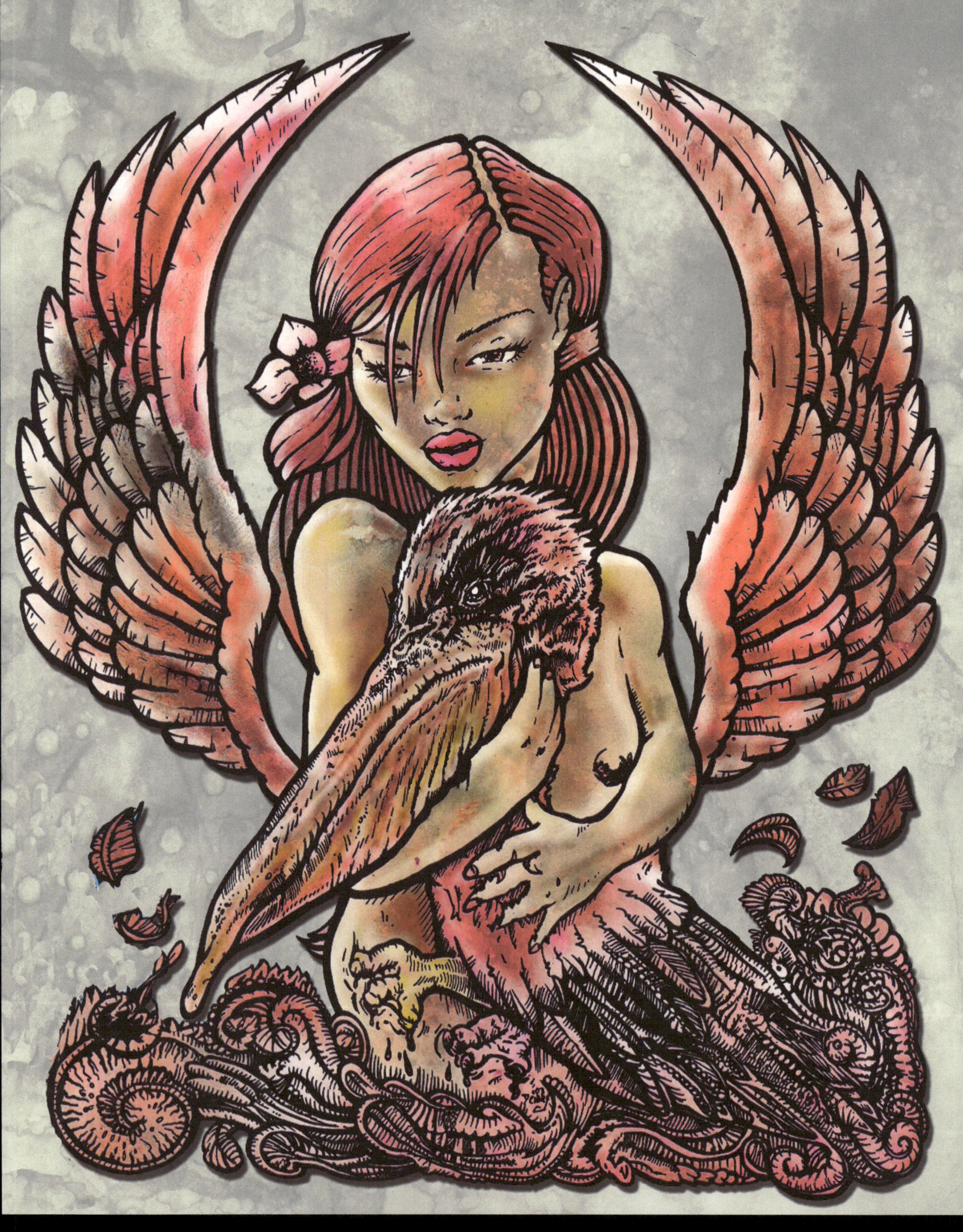

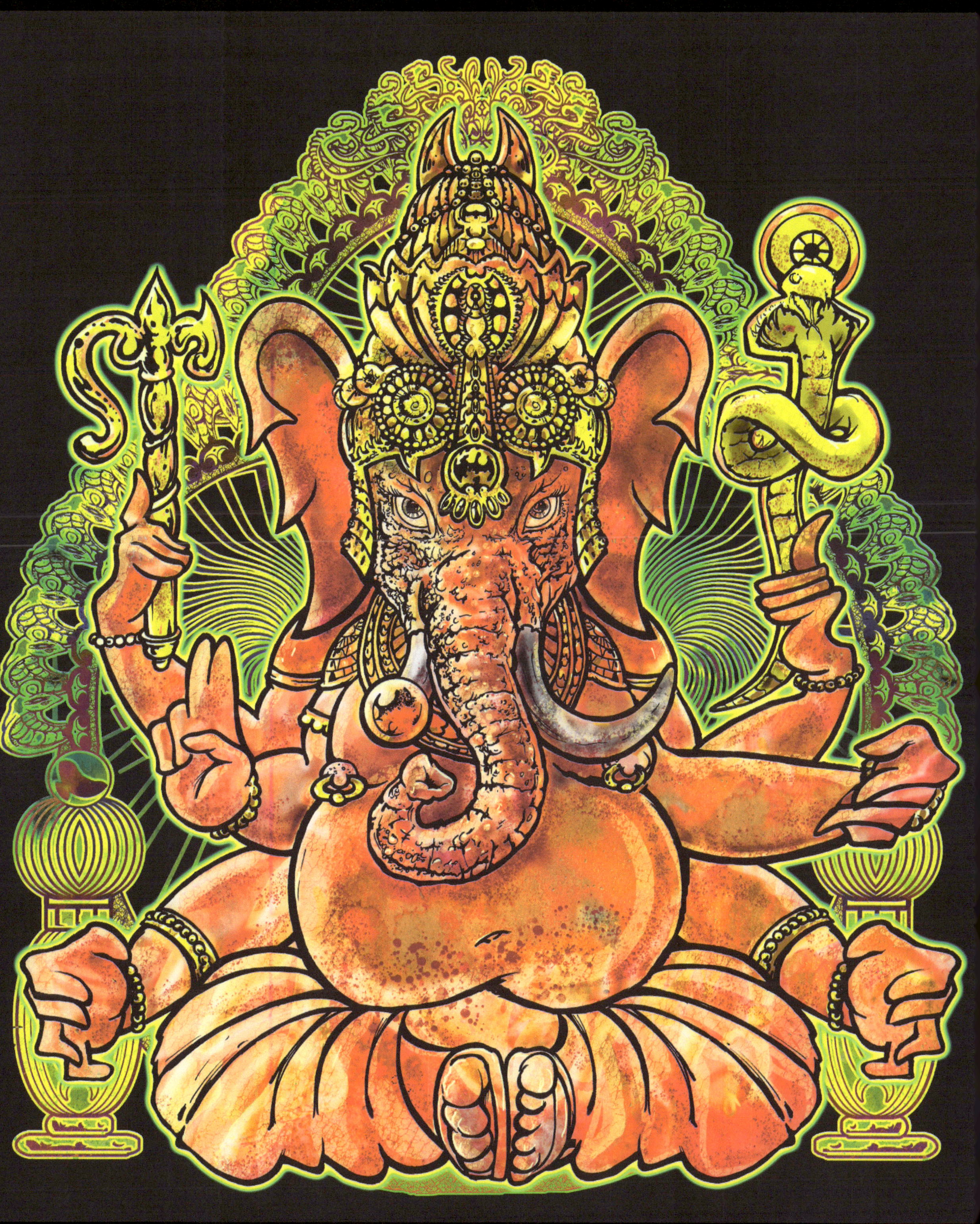

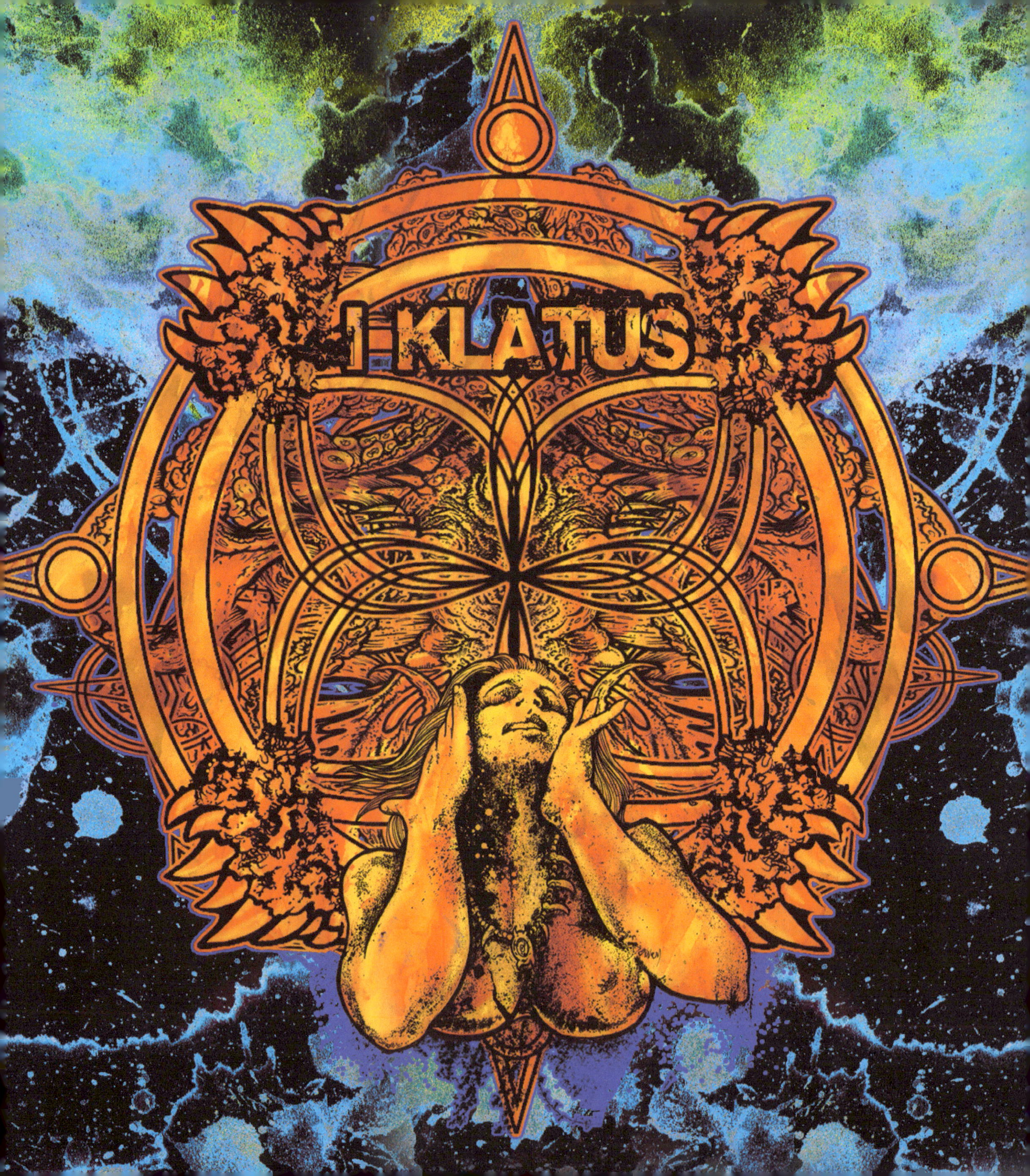
I KLATUS

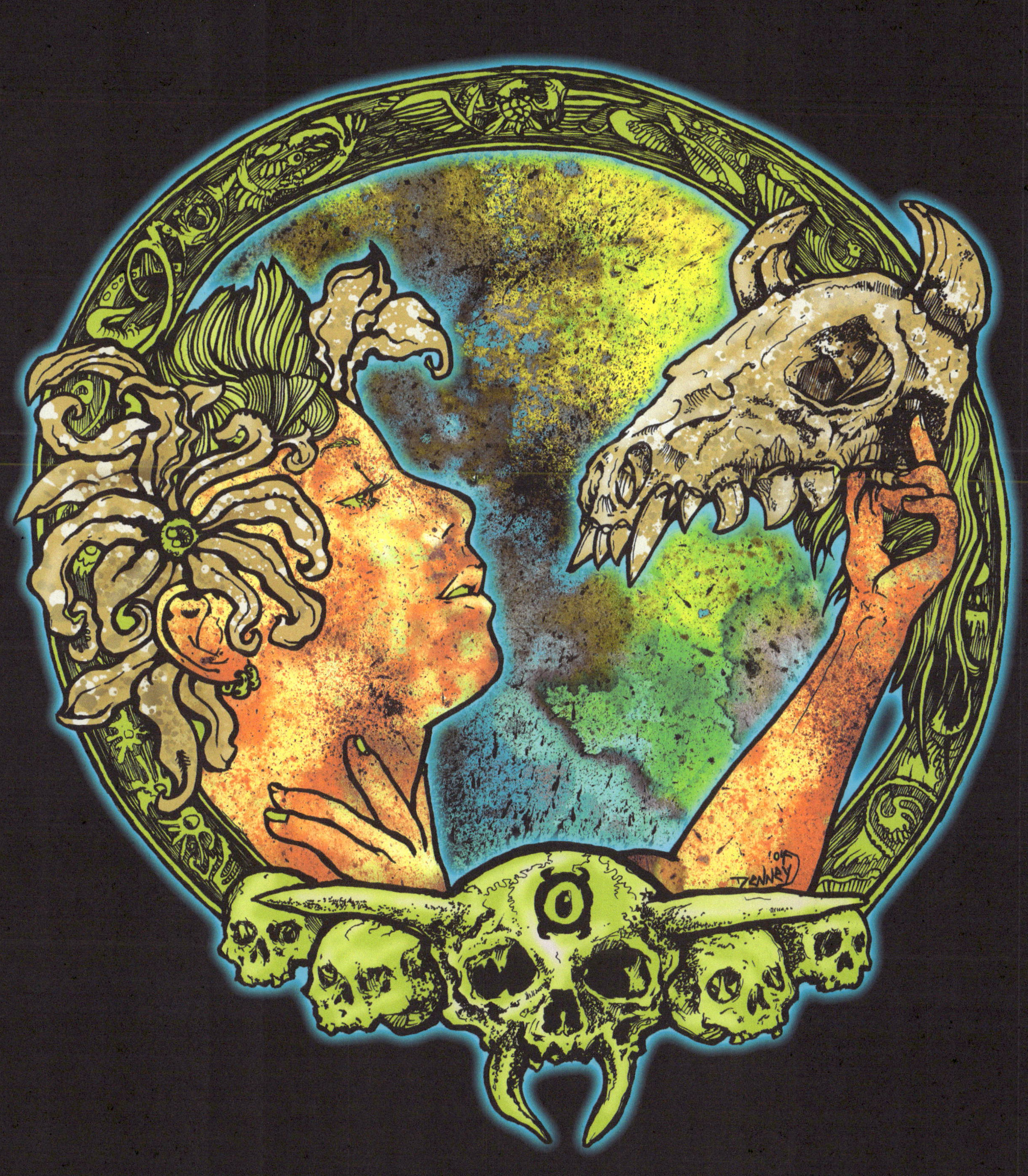

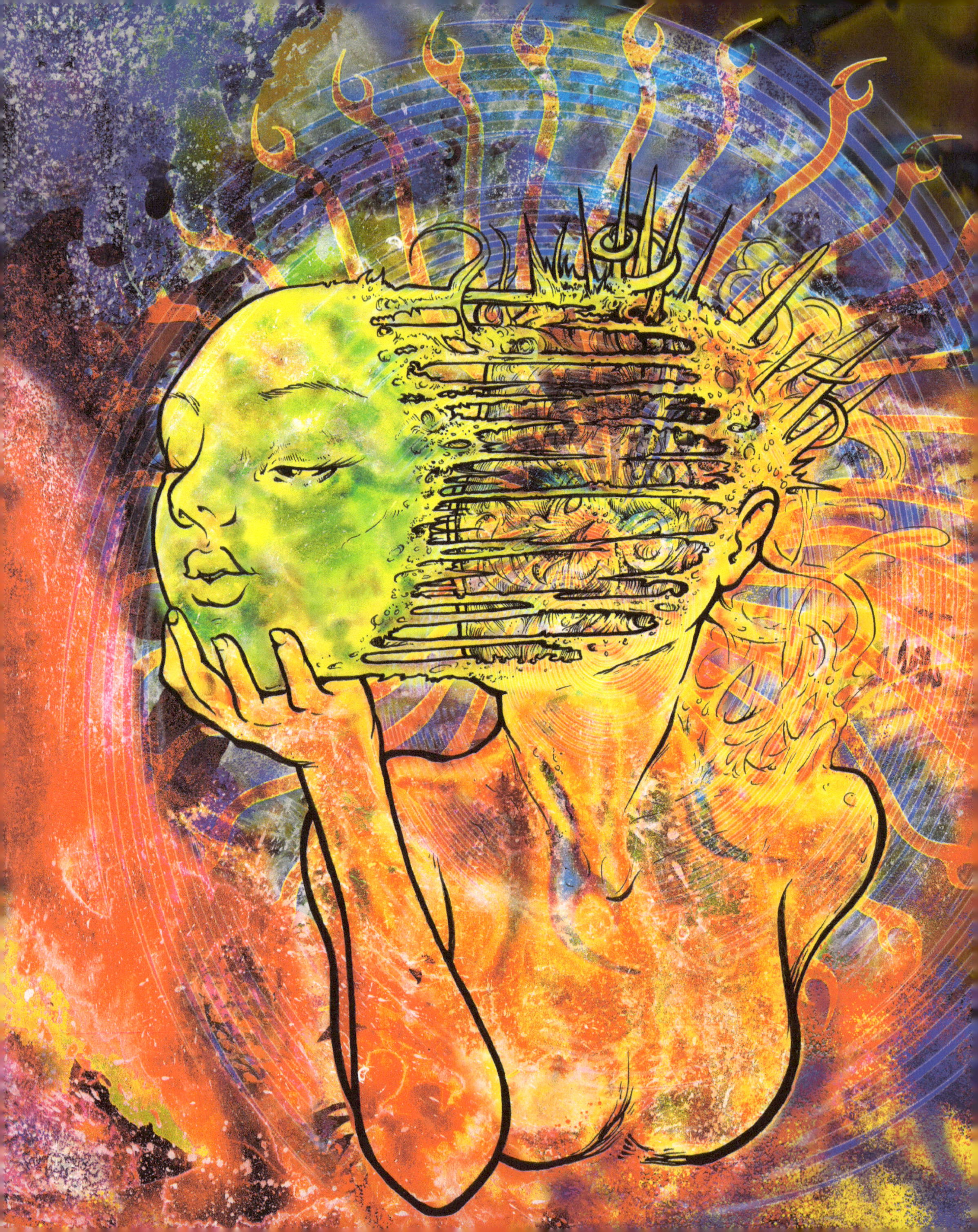

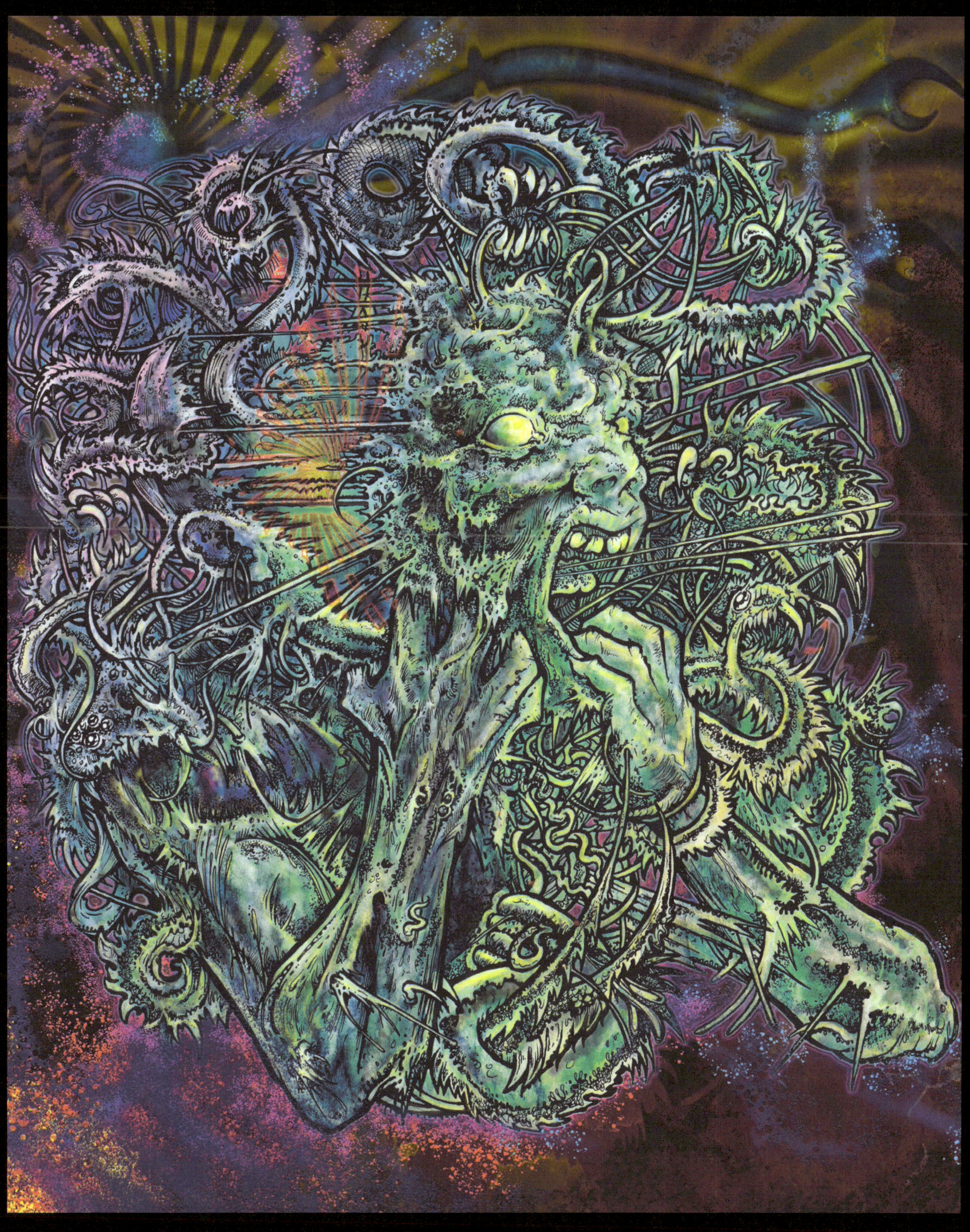

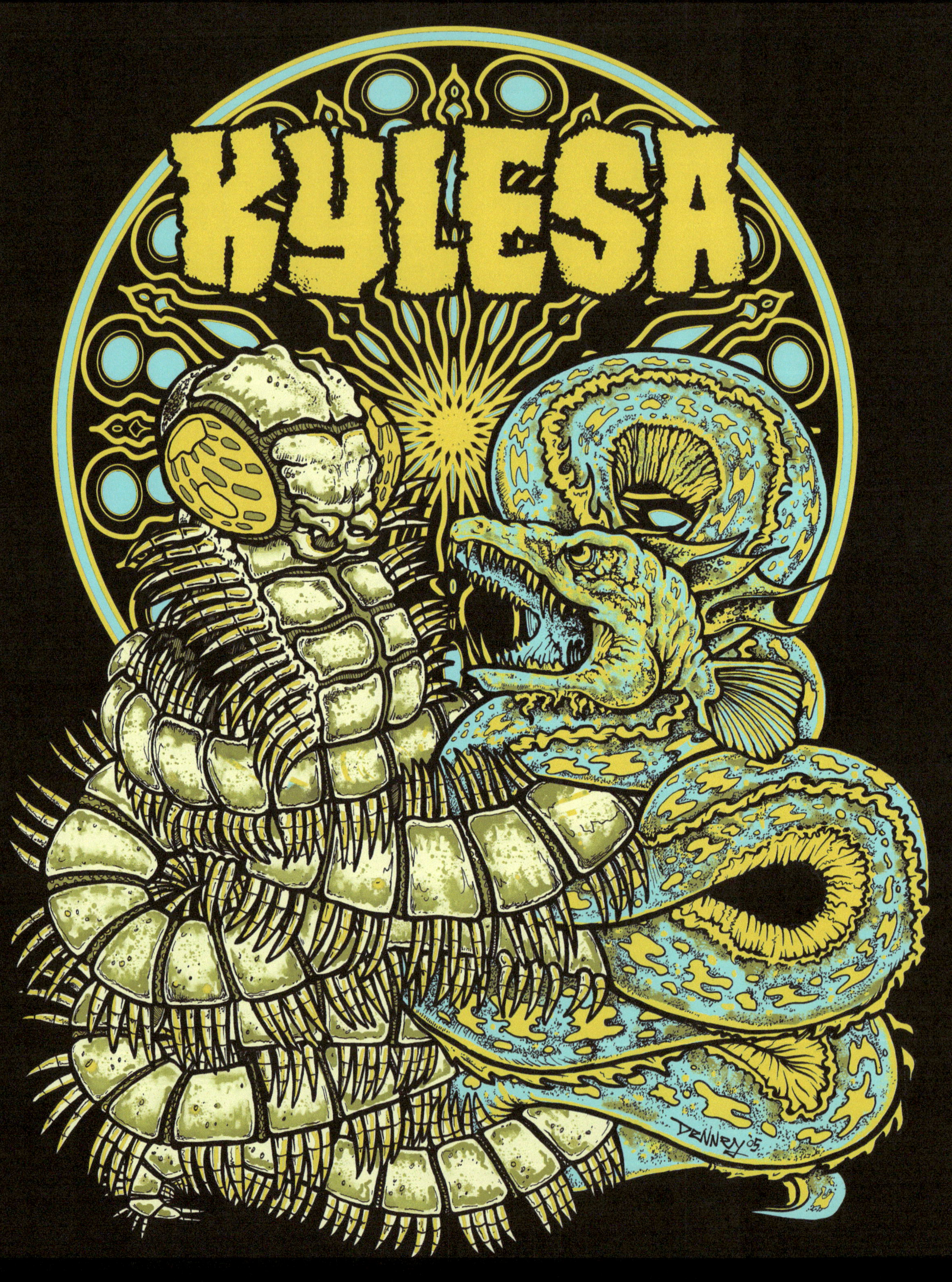
KYLESA
DENNEY '05

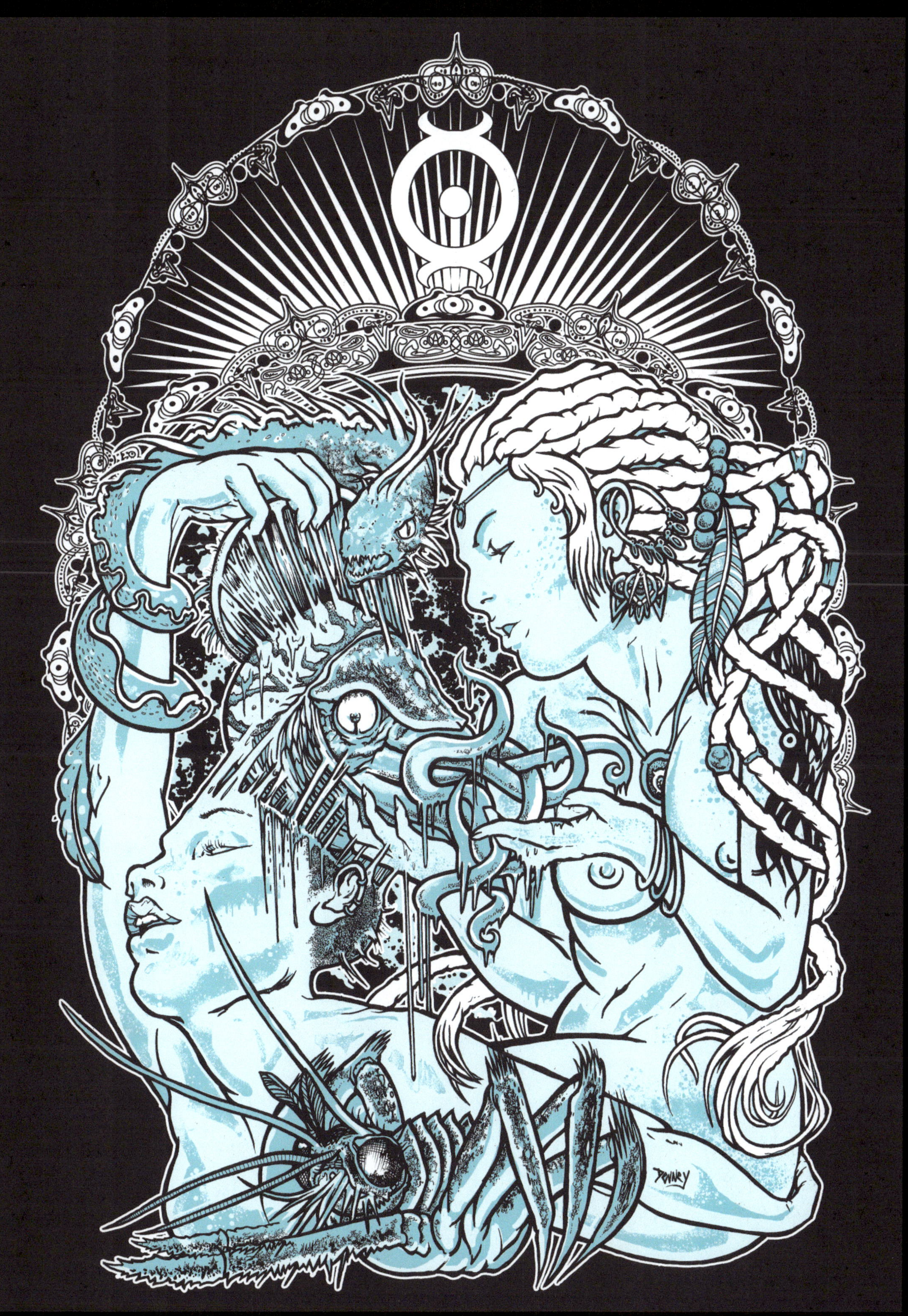

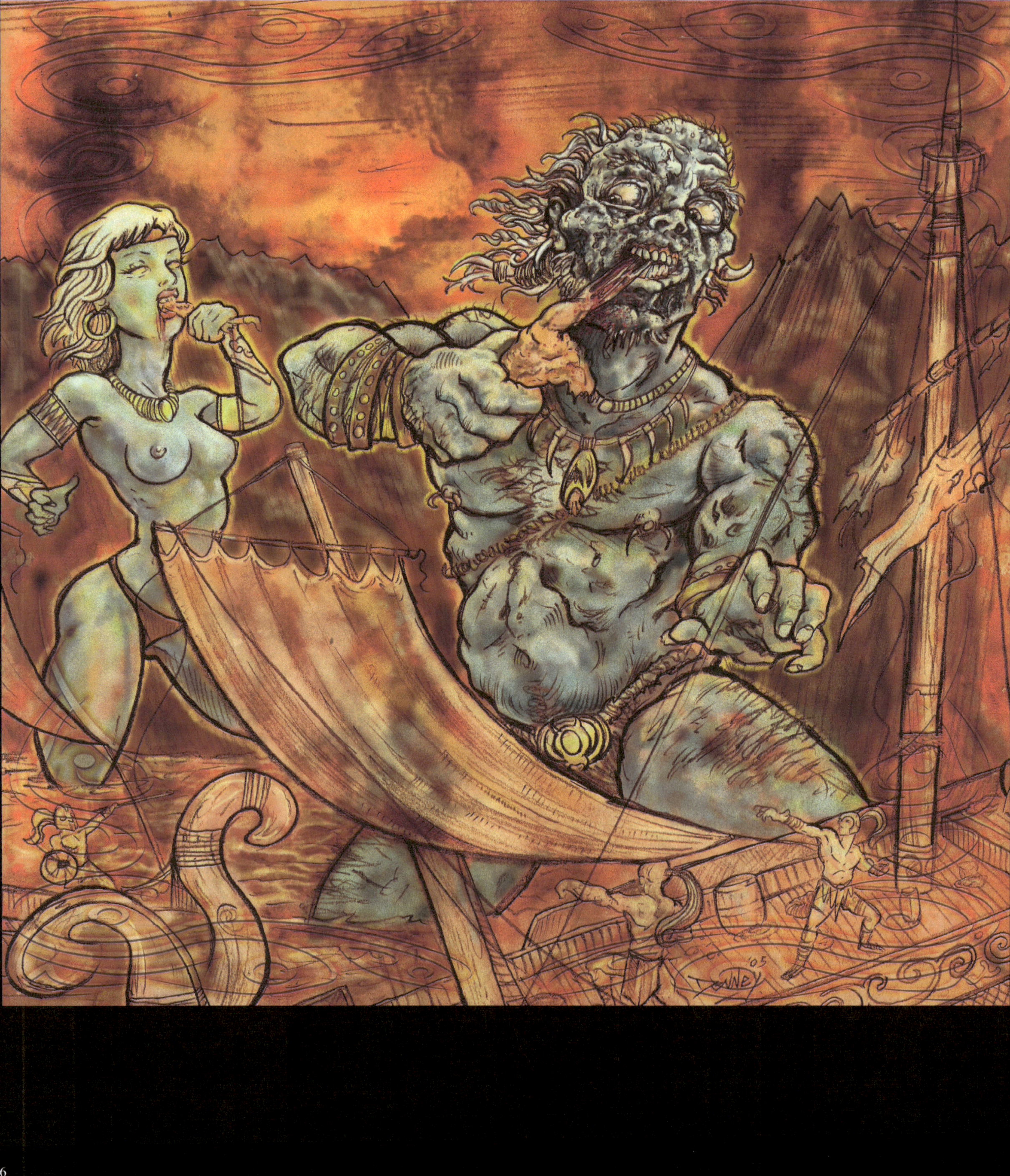

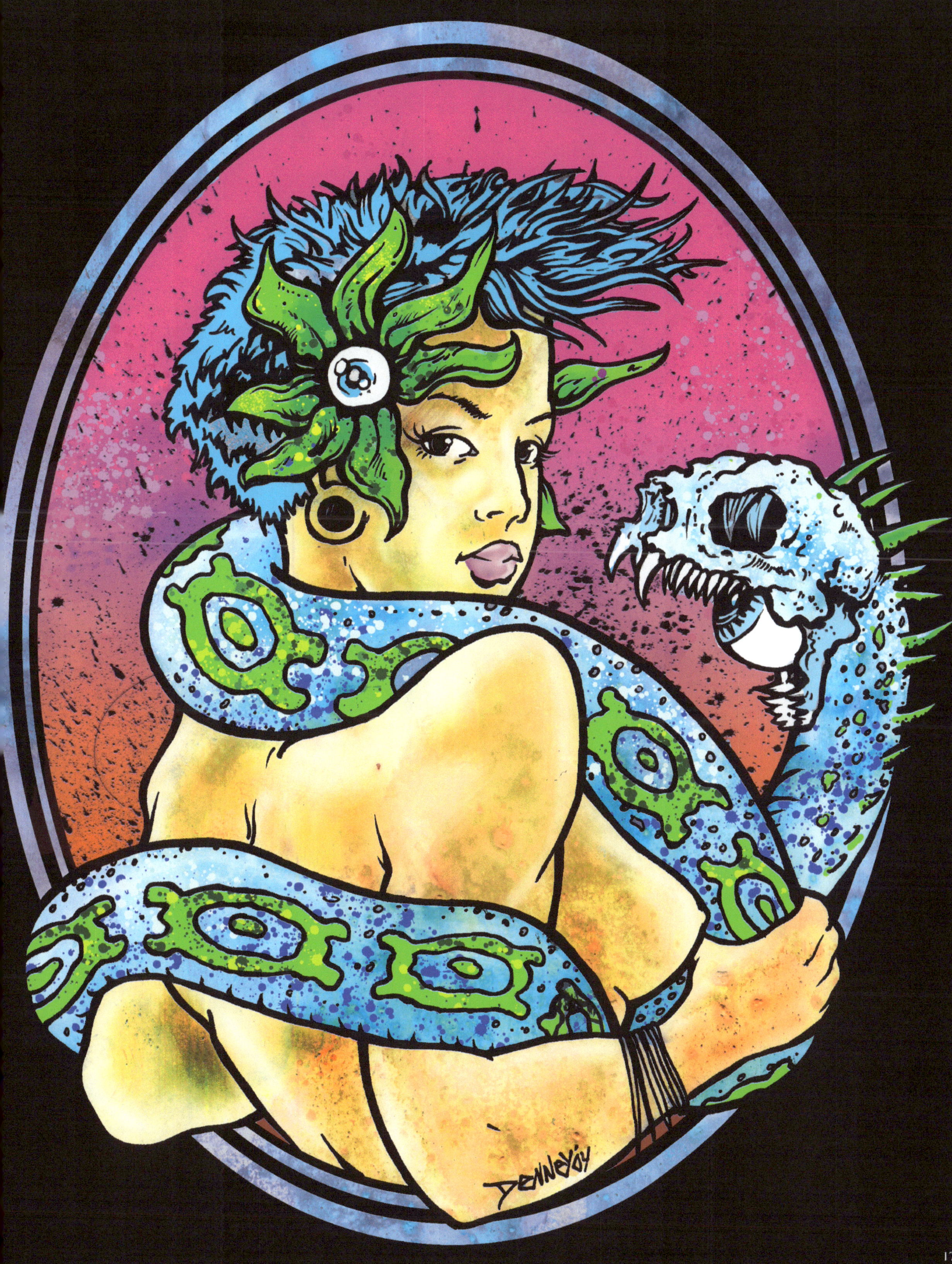
Denney'04

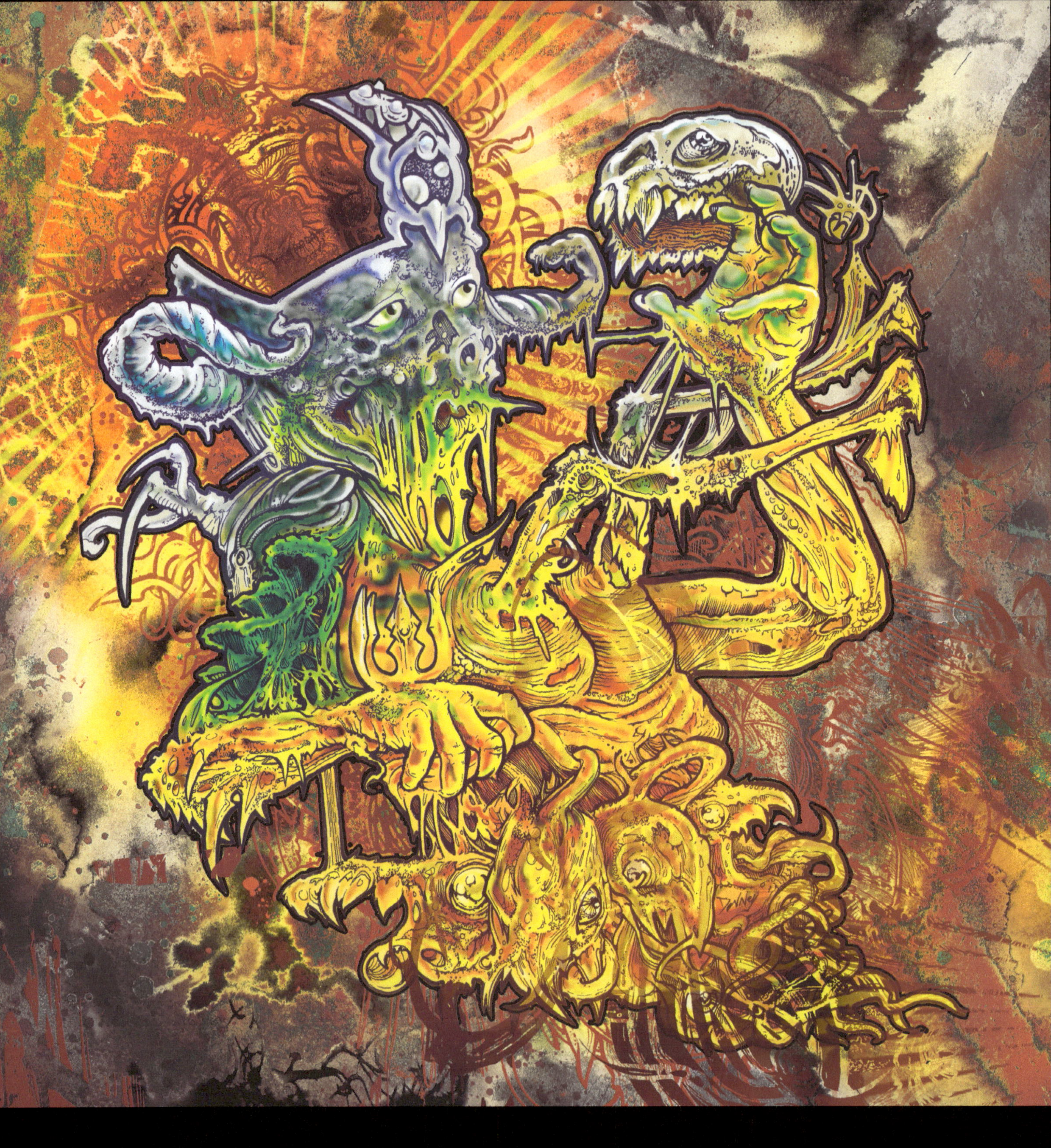

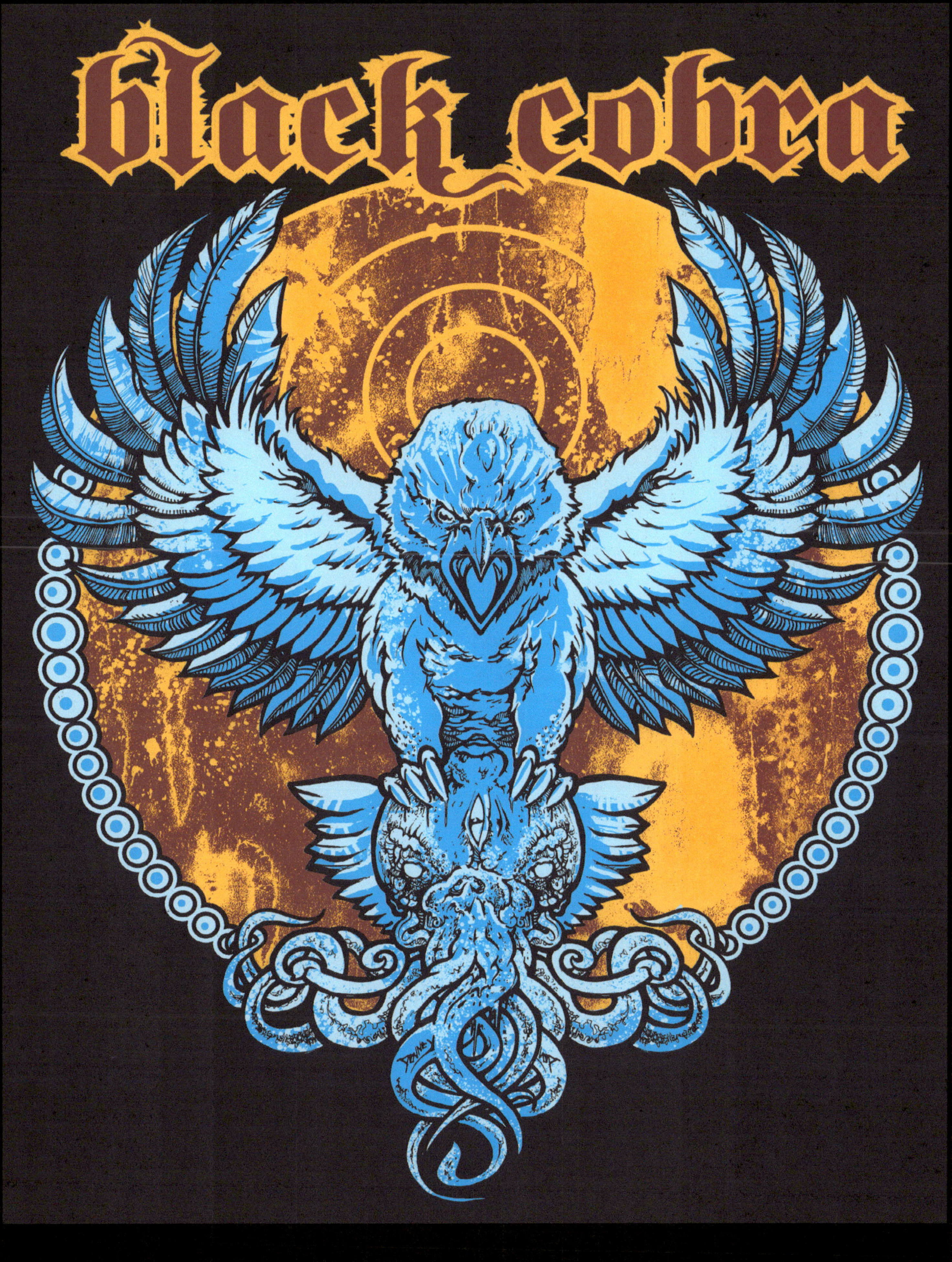

black cobra

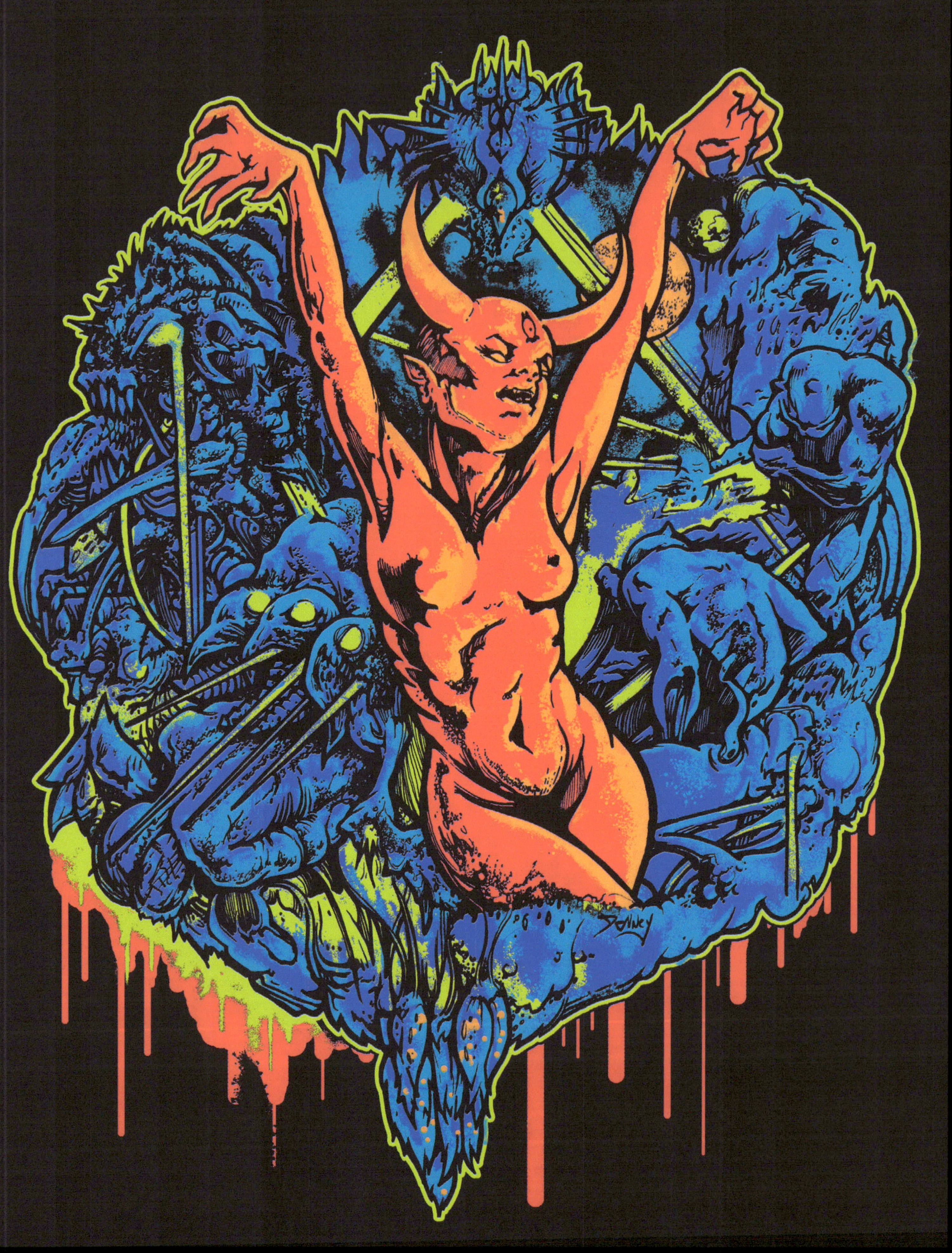

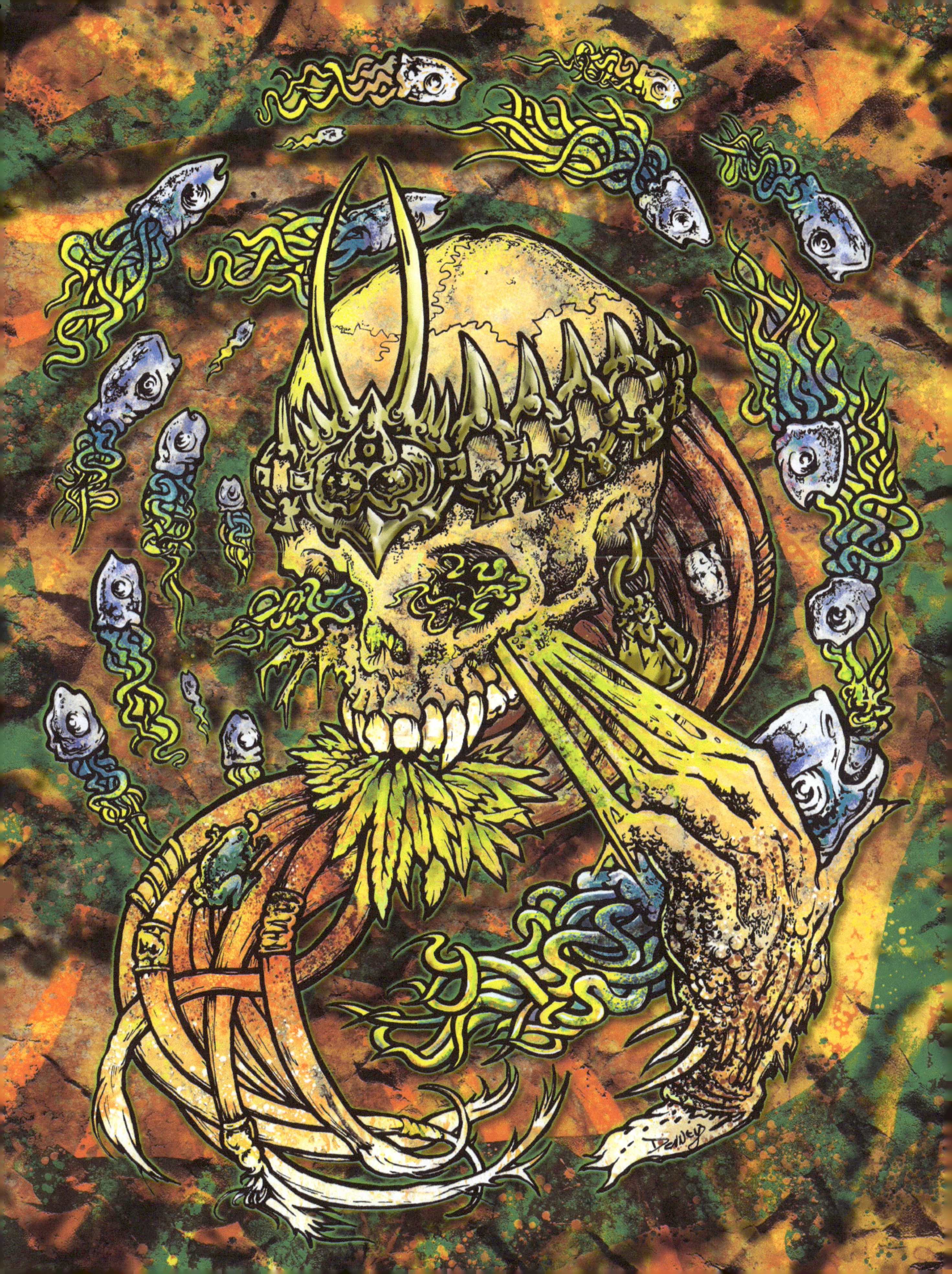

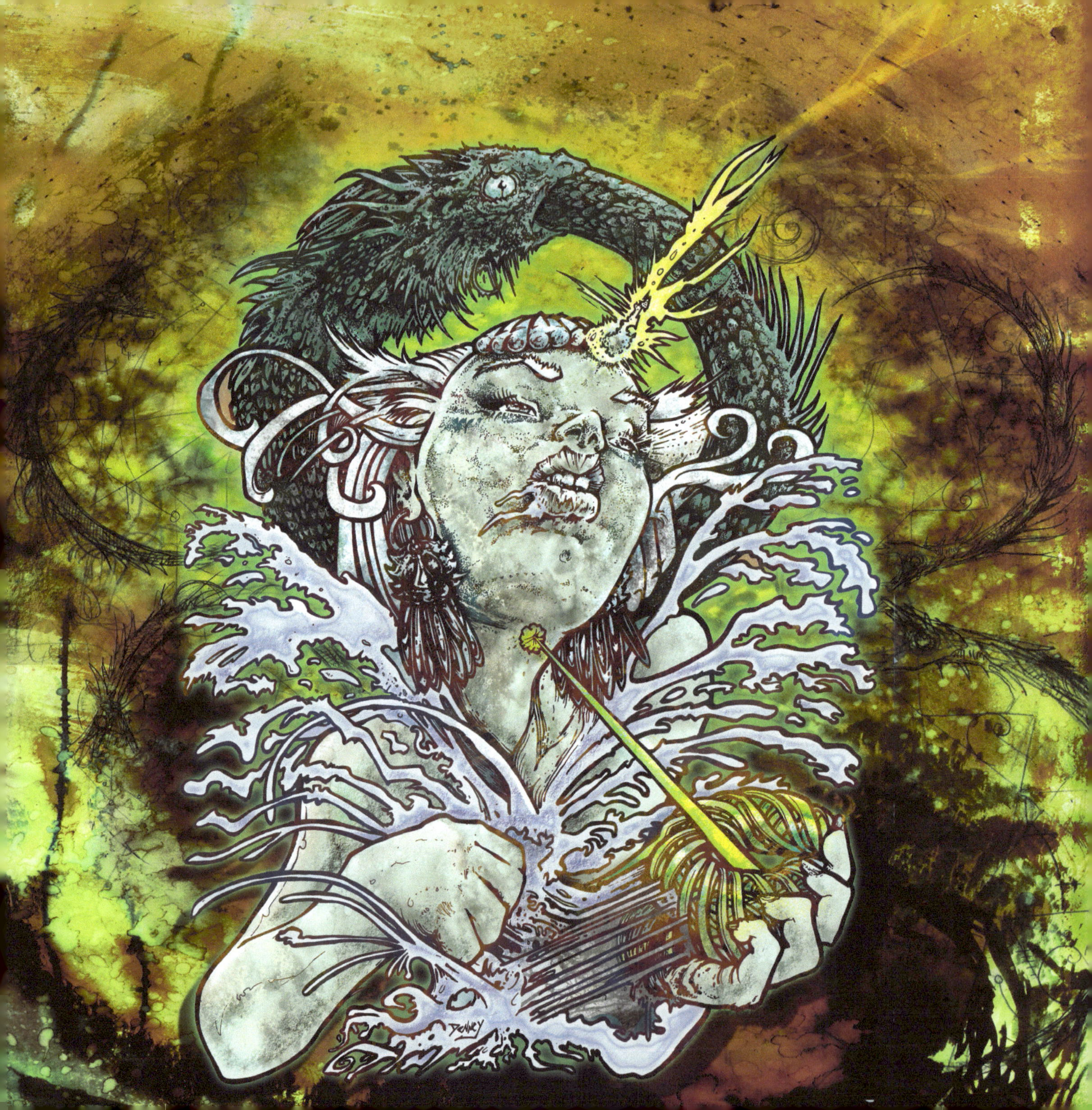

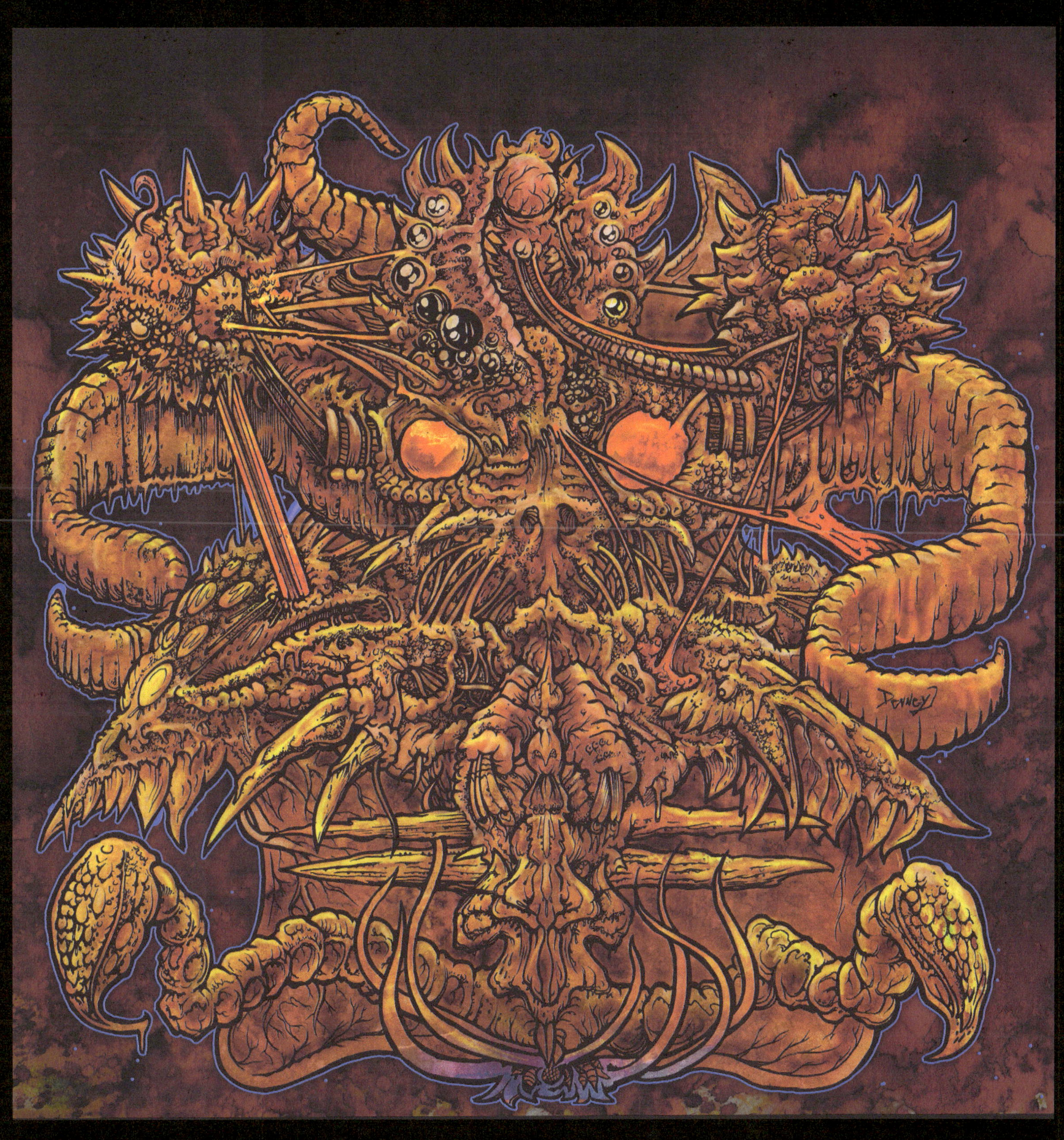

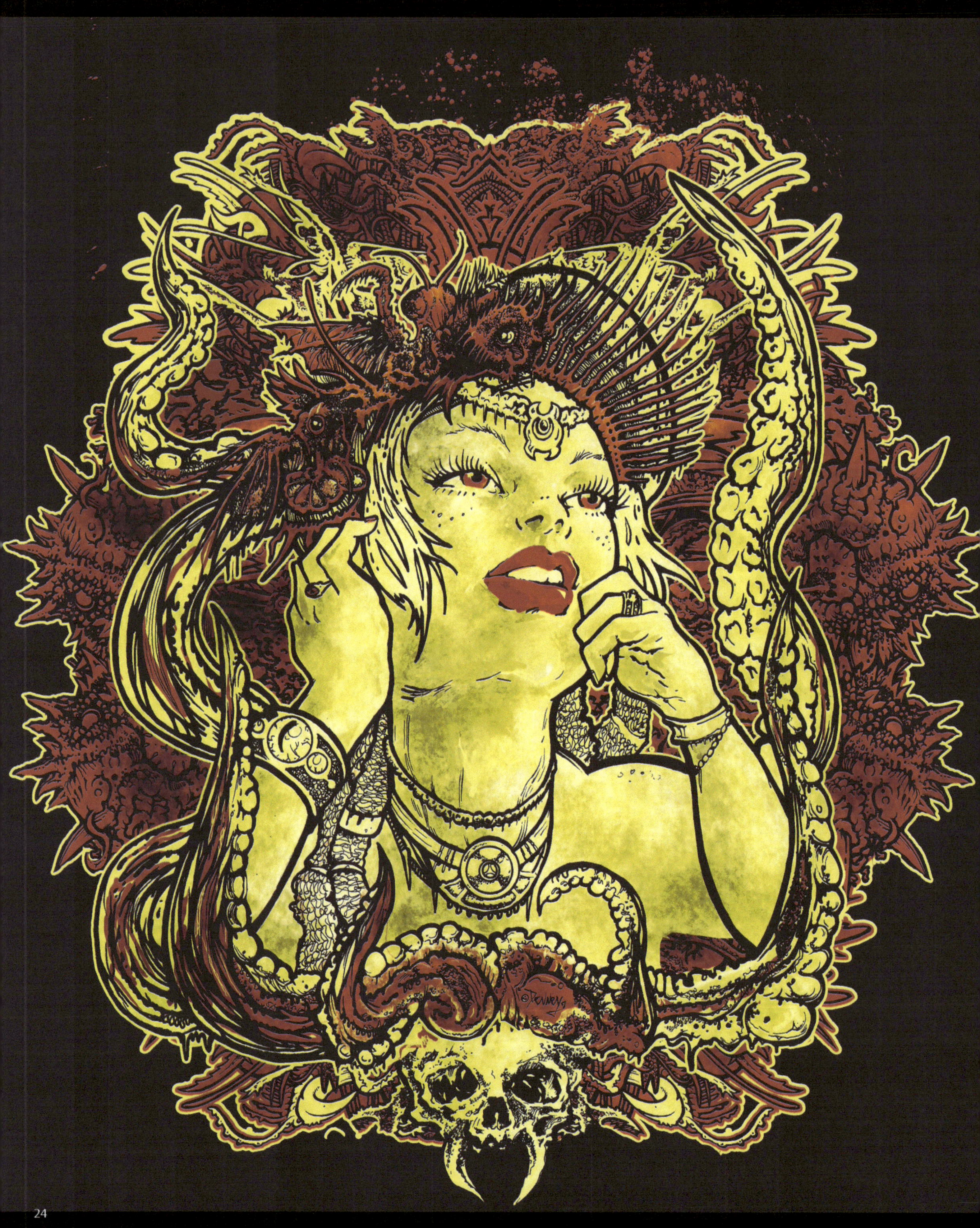

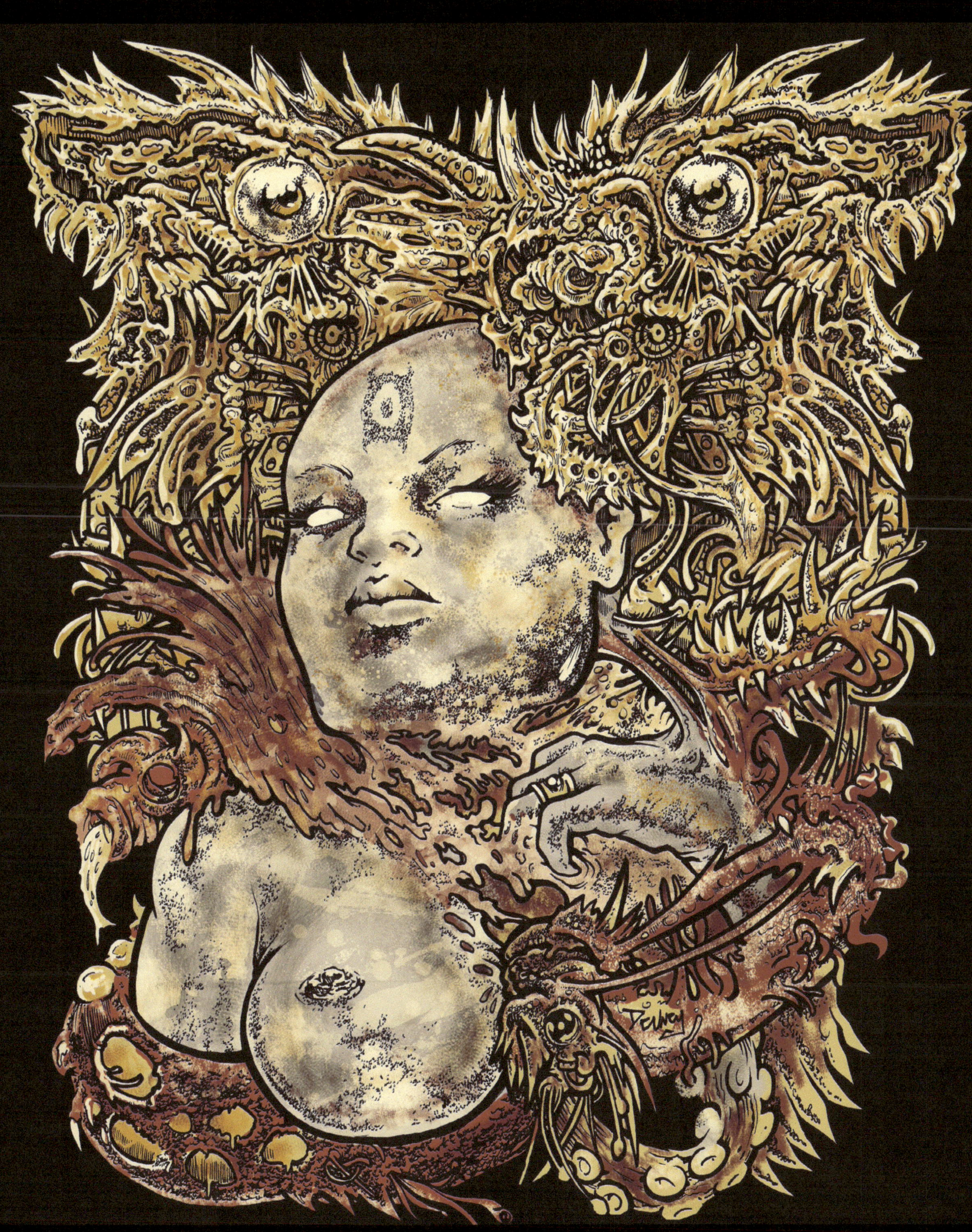

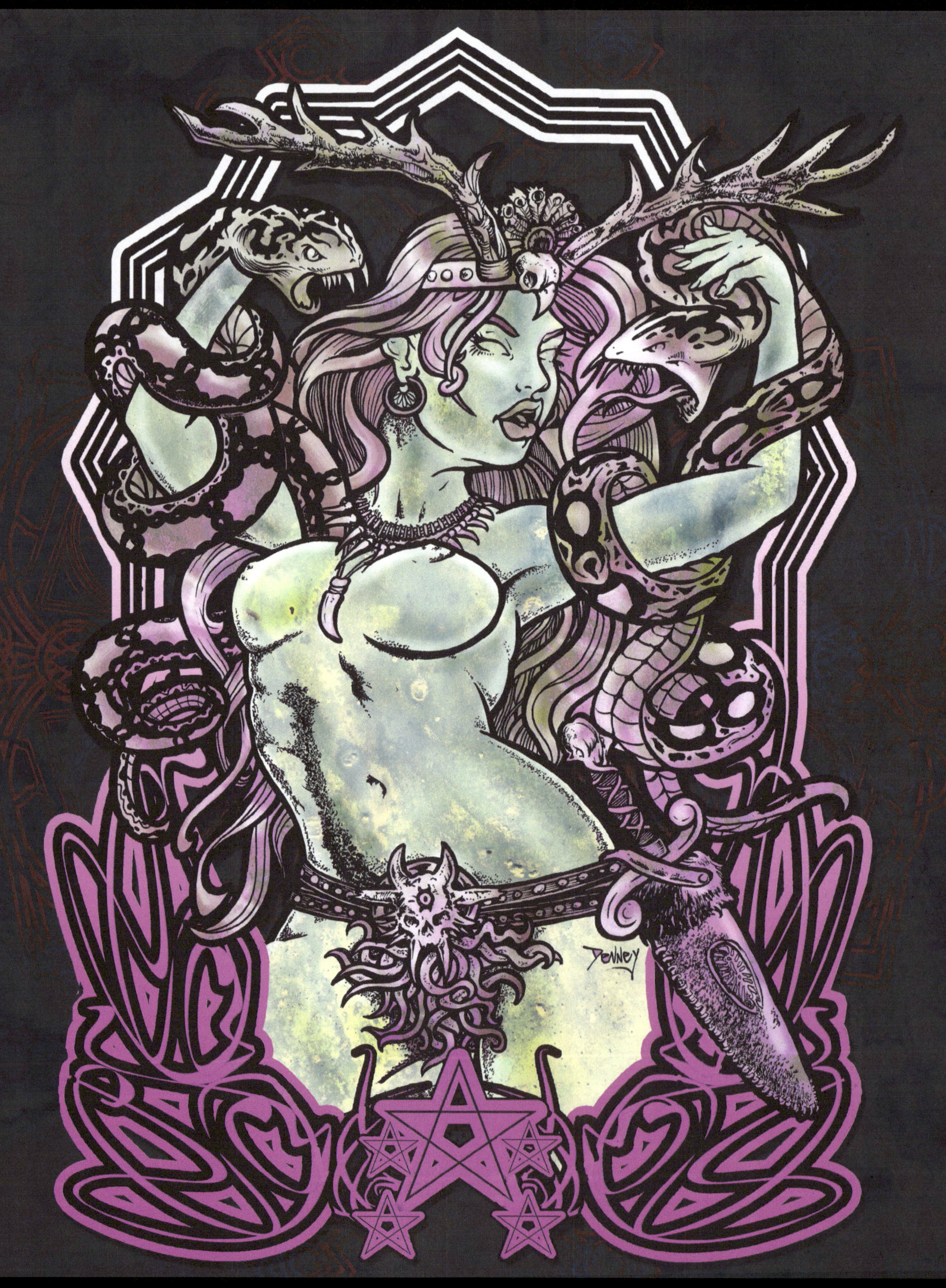
DENNEY

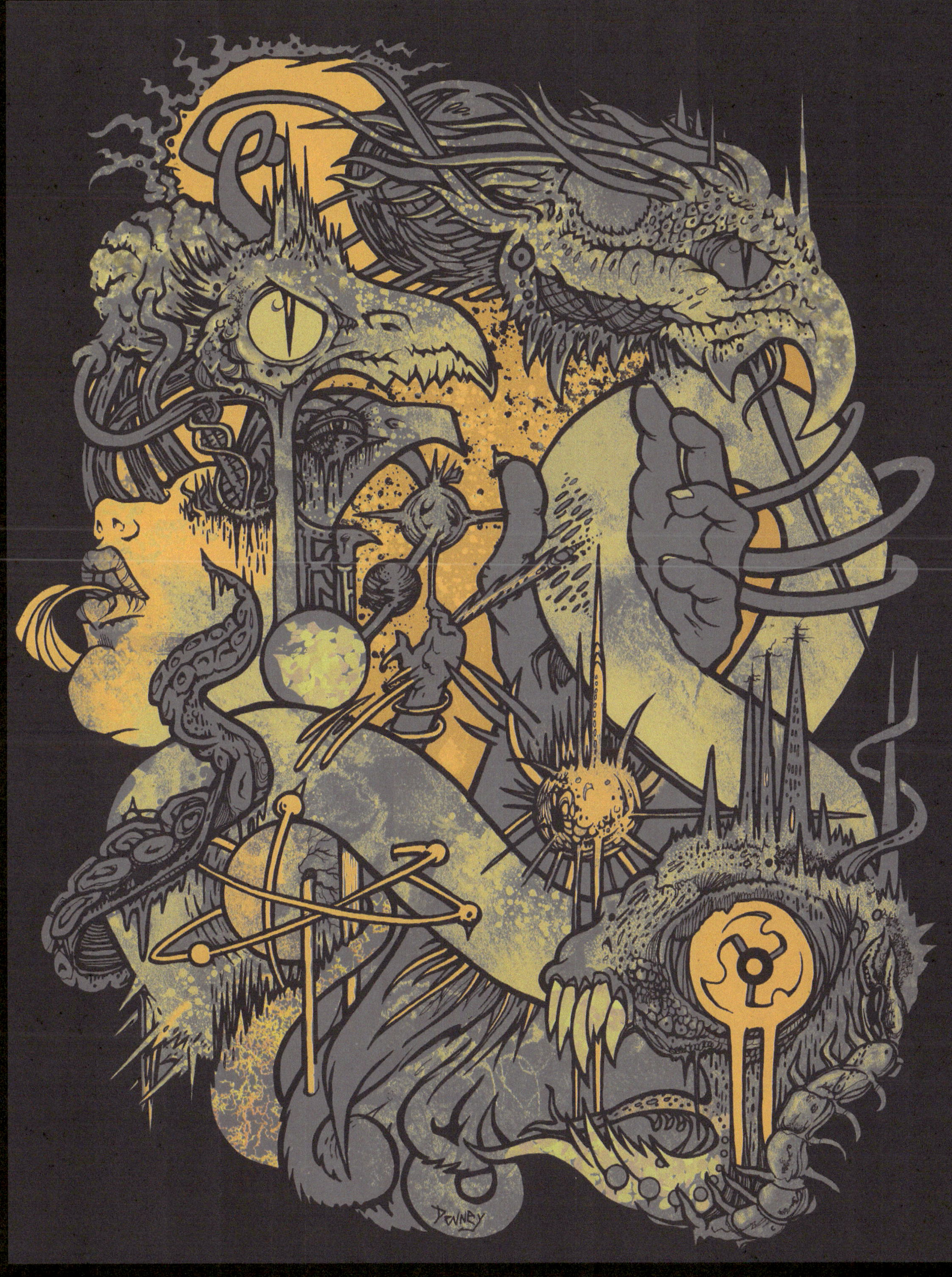
DOWNEY

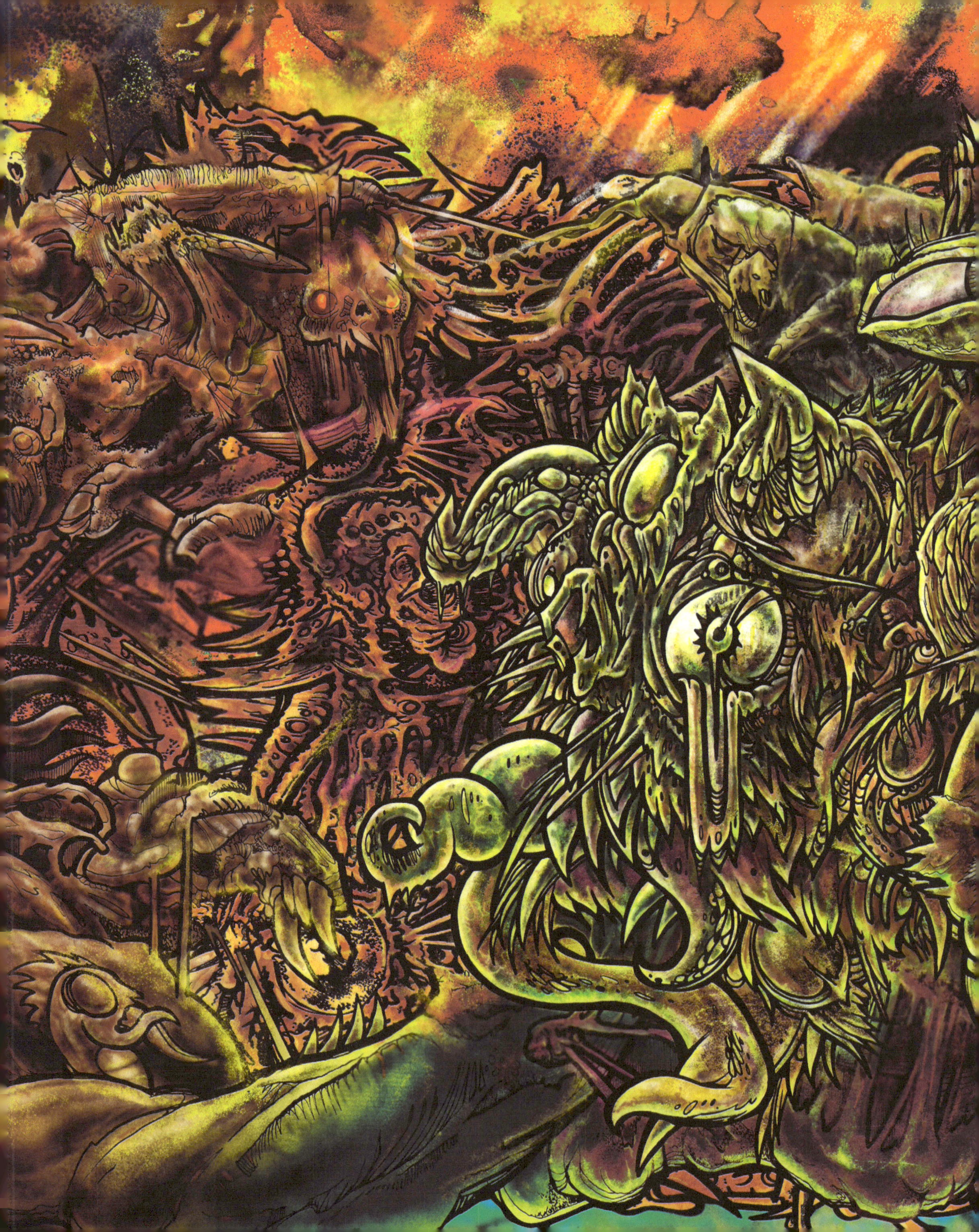

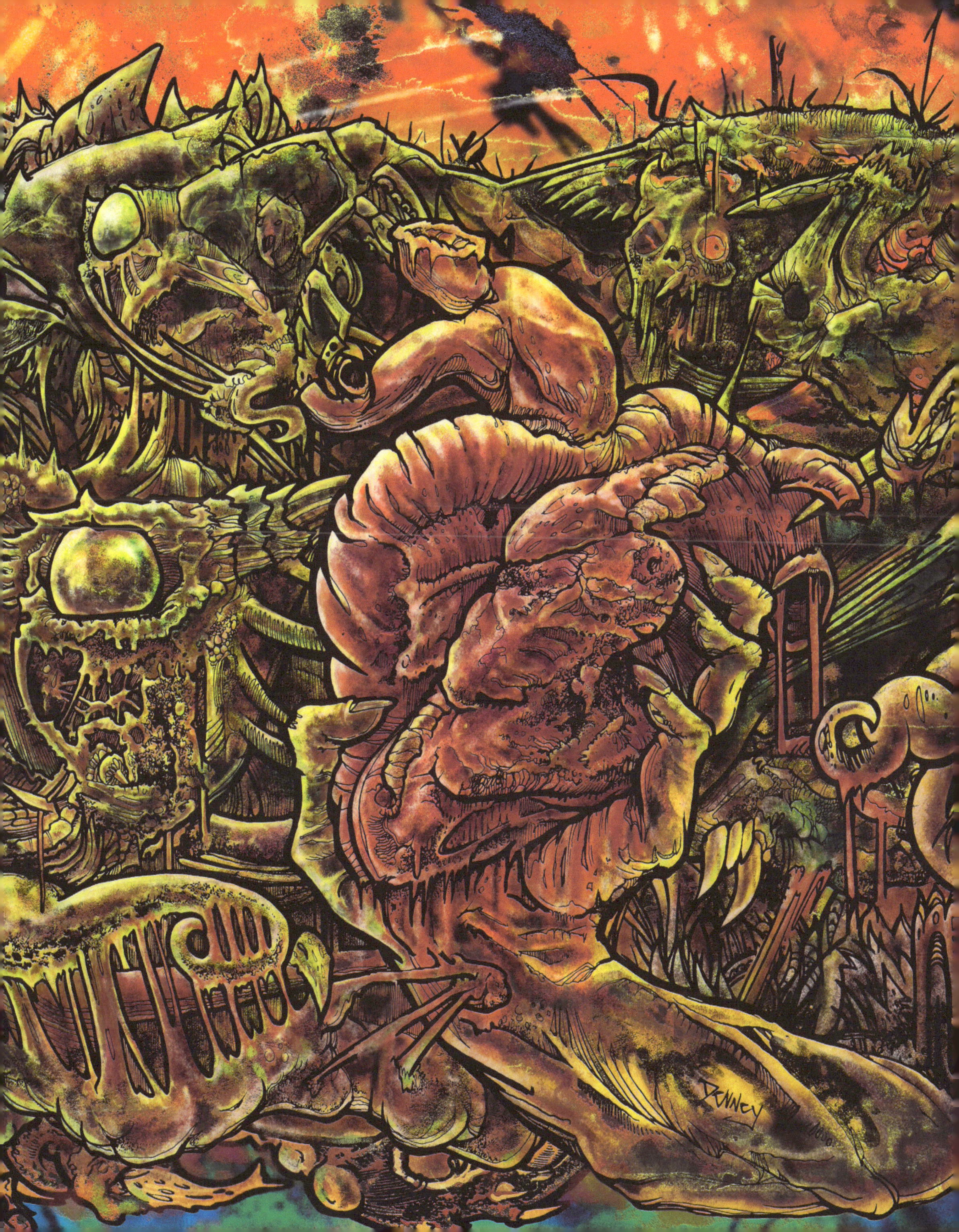
DENNEY

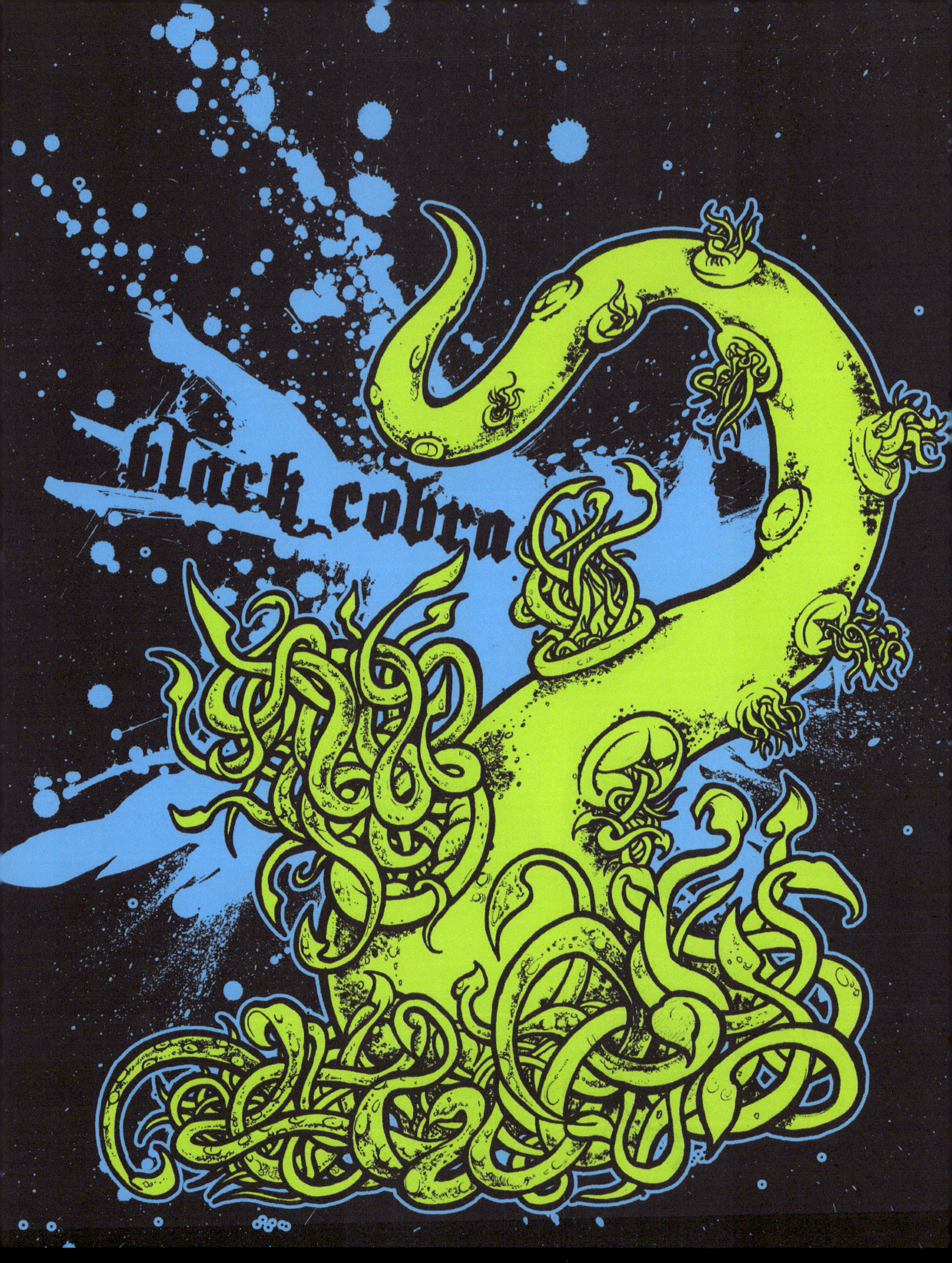
black cobra

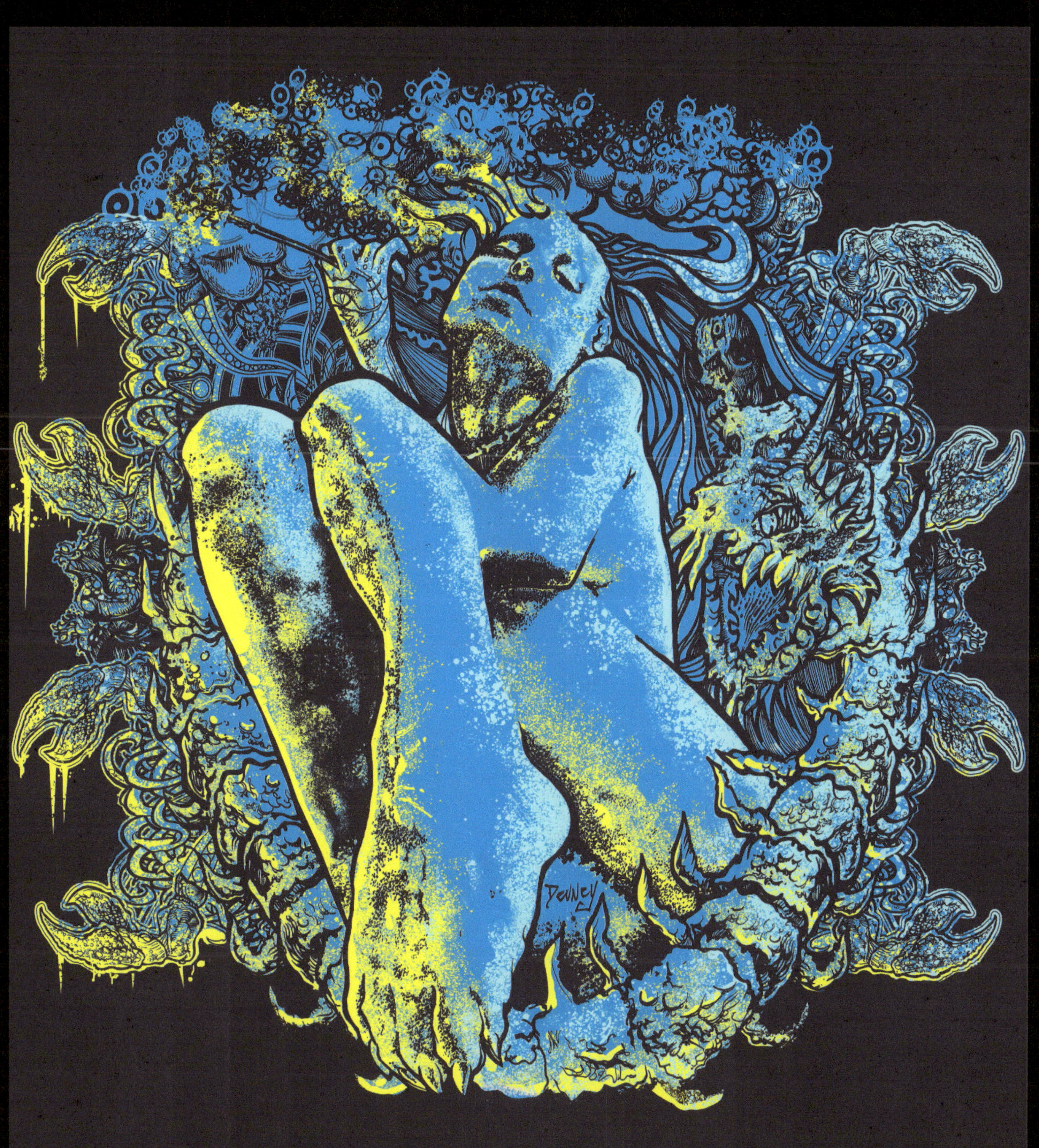
Dewey

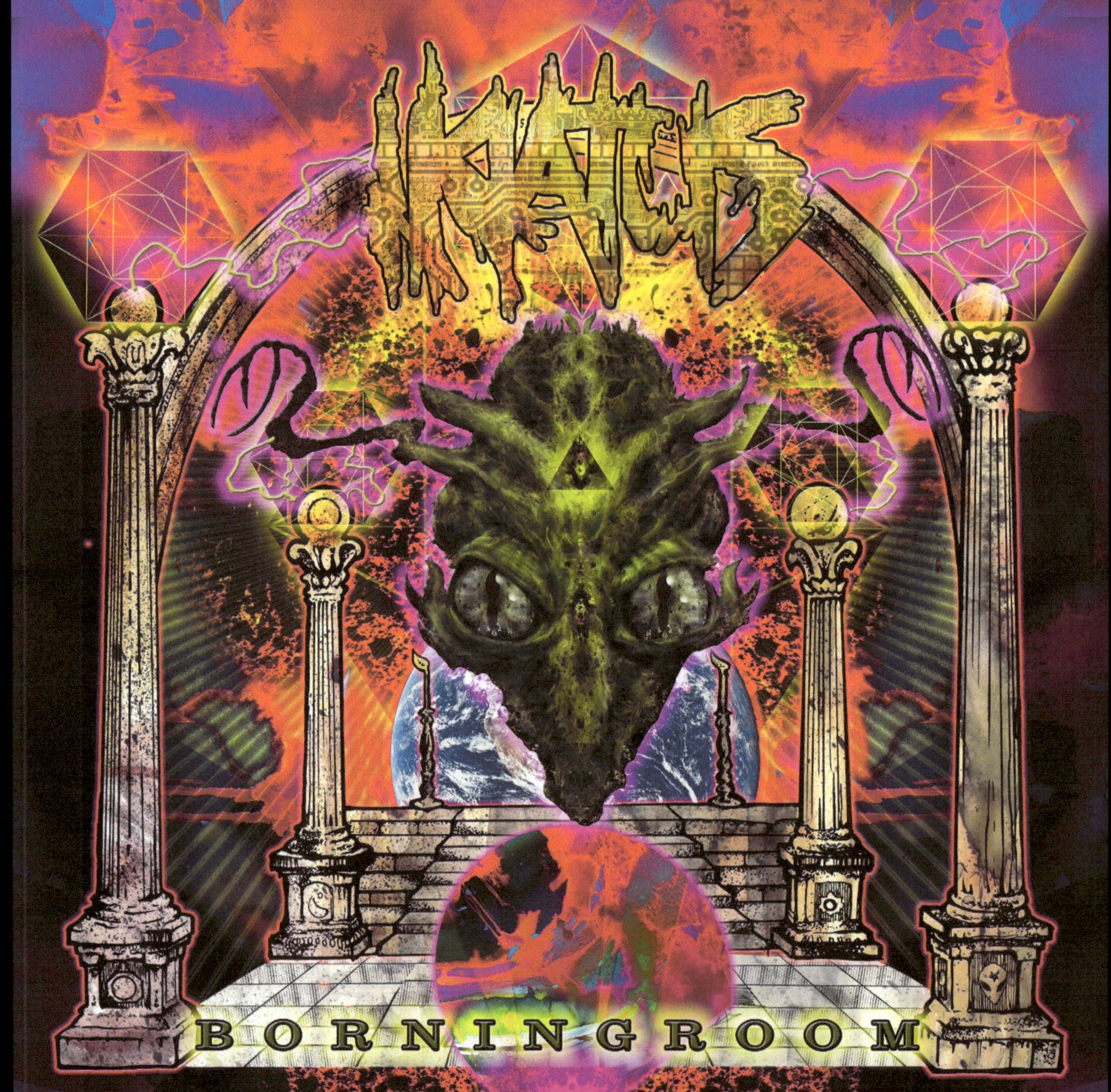
BORNINGROOM

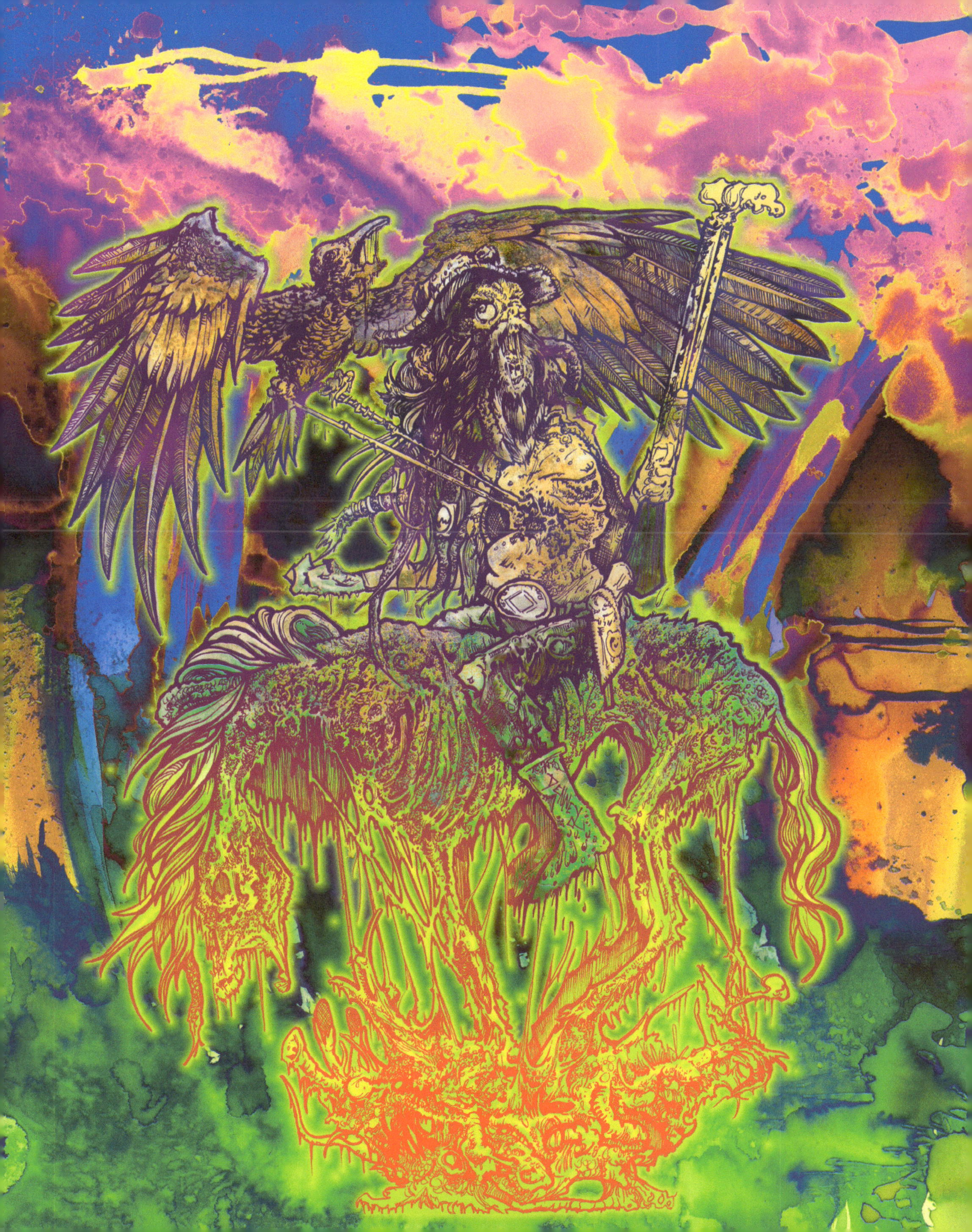

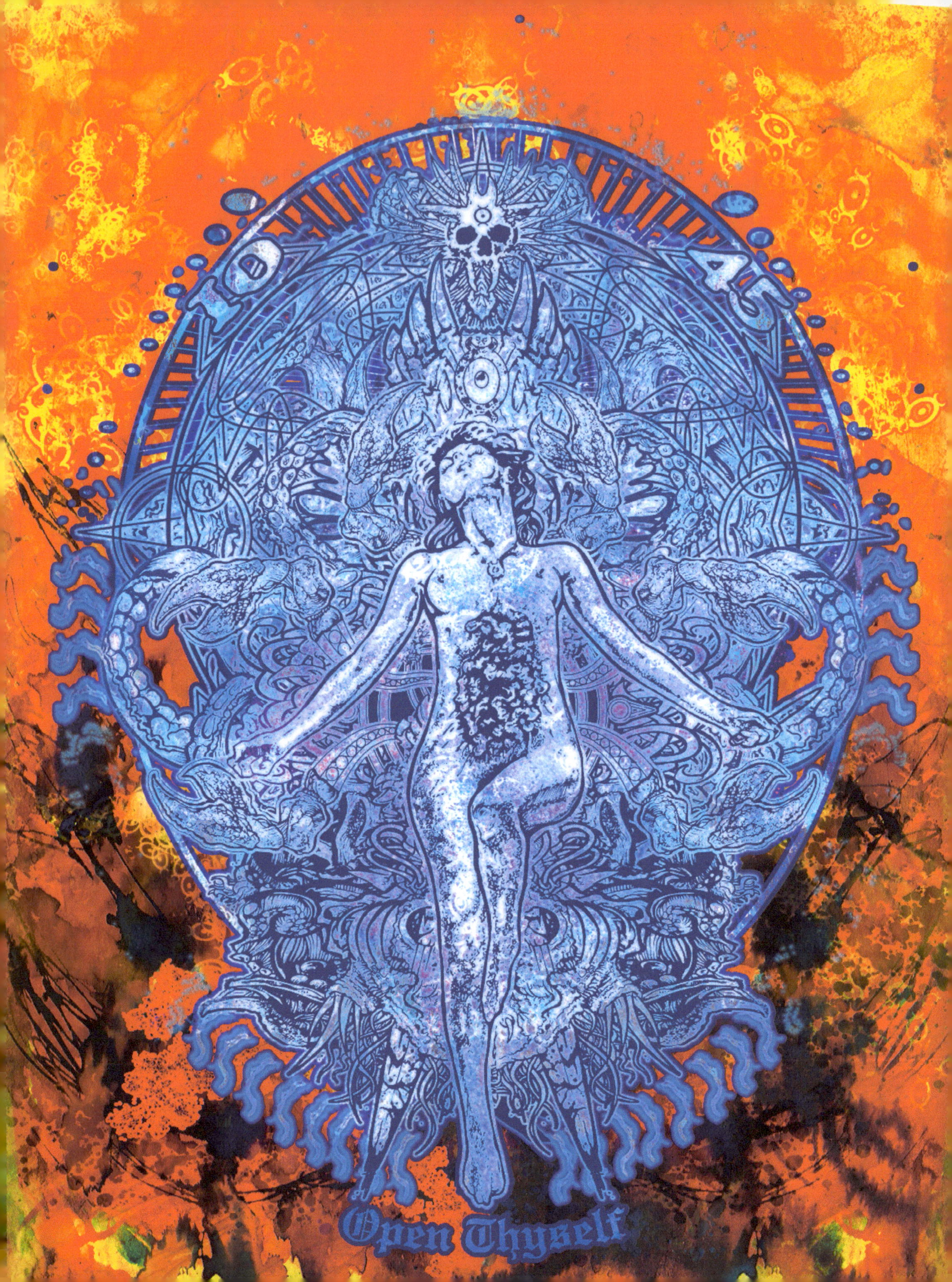
Open Thyself

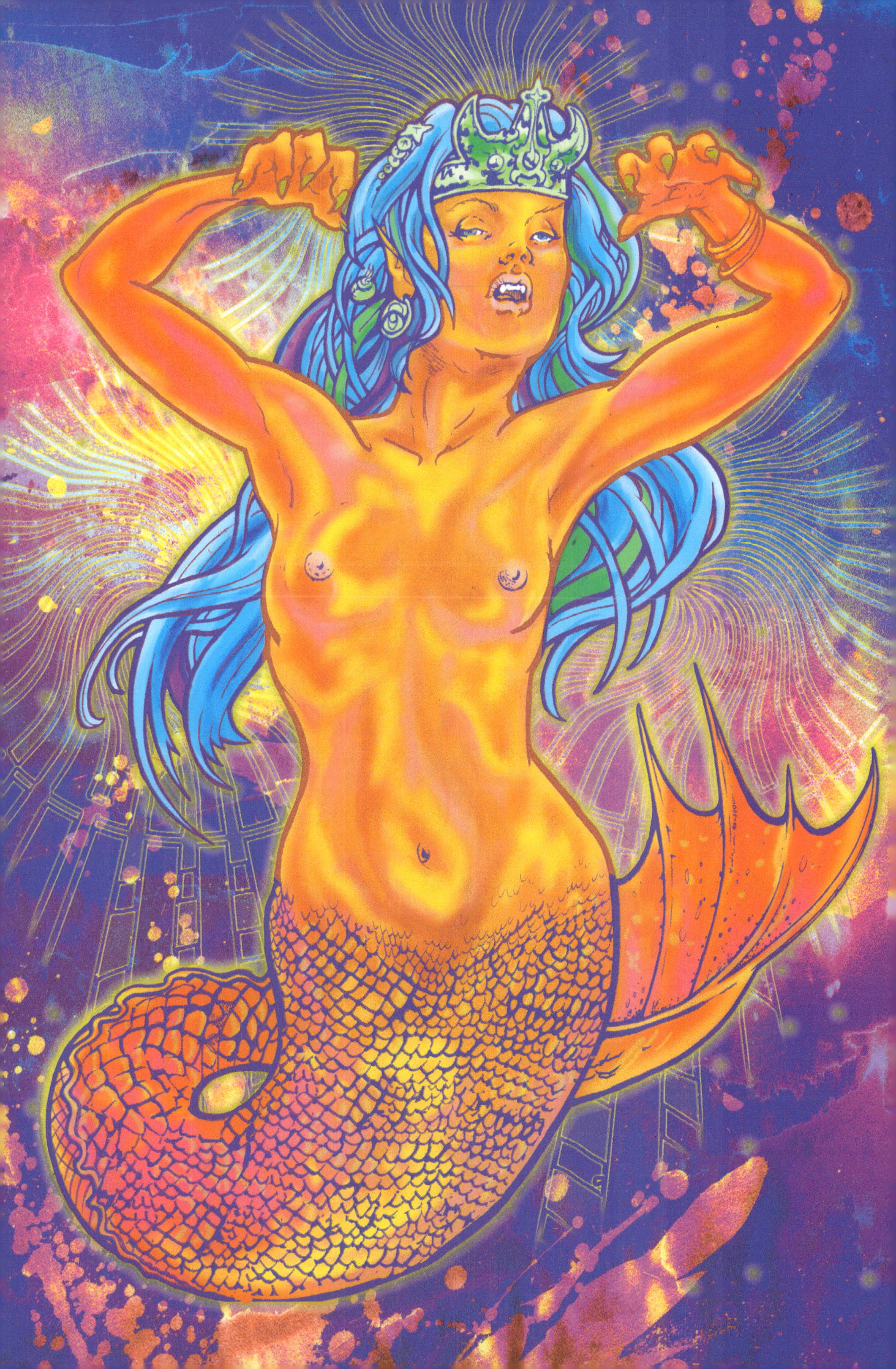

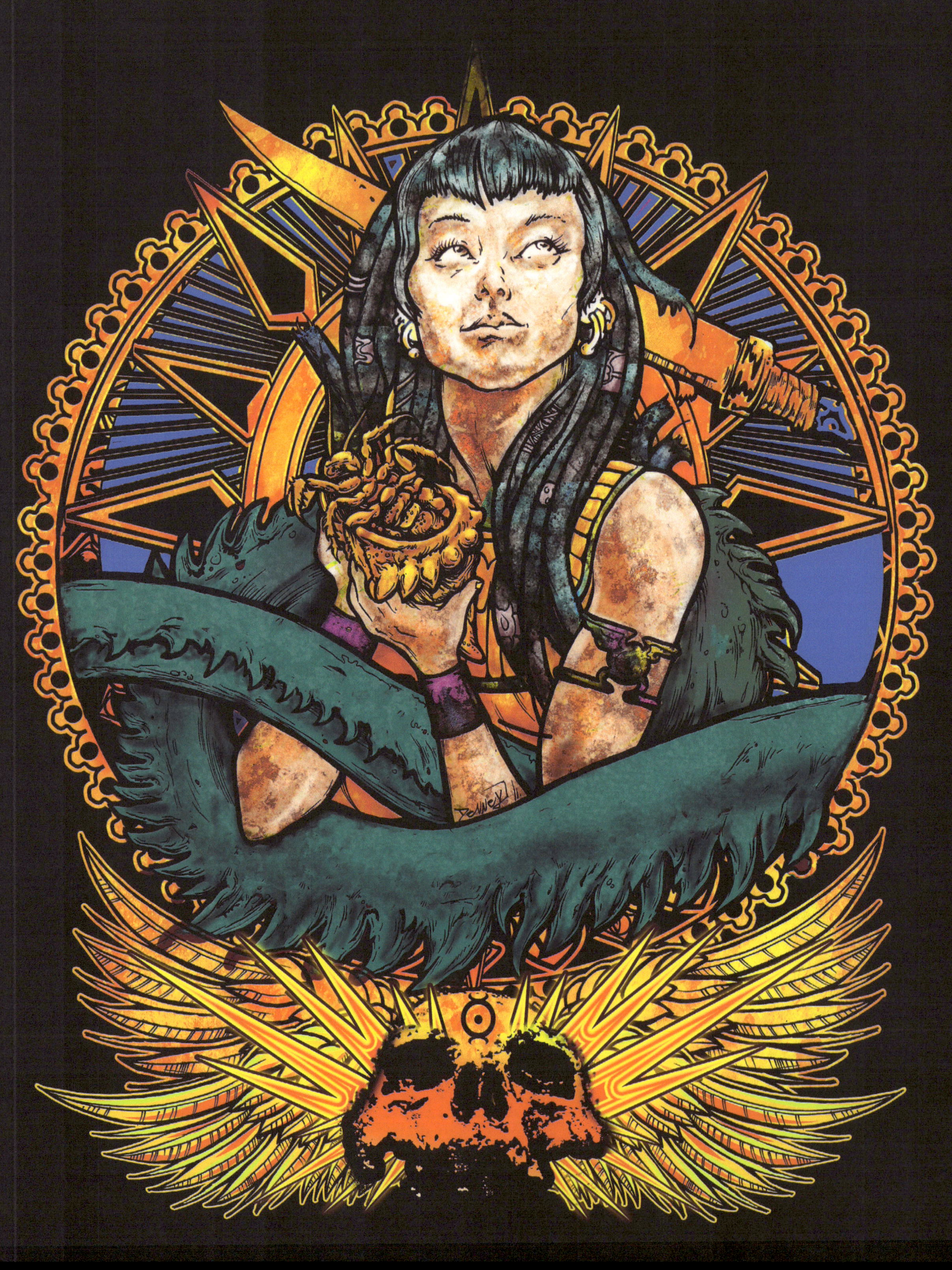

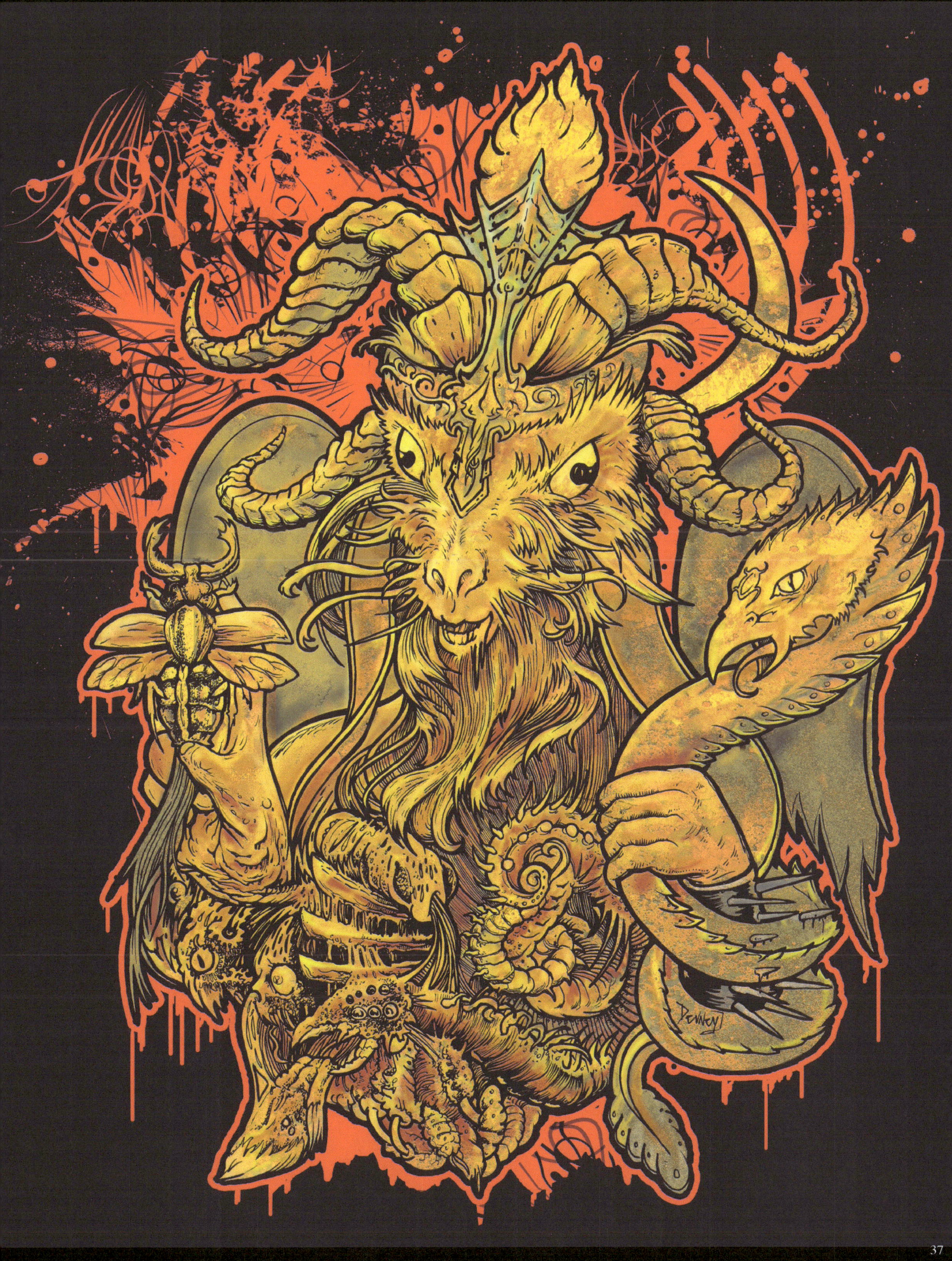

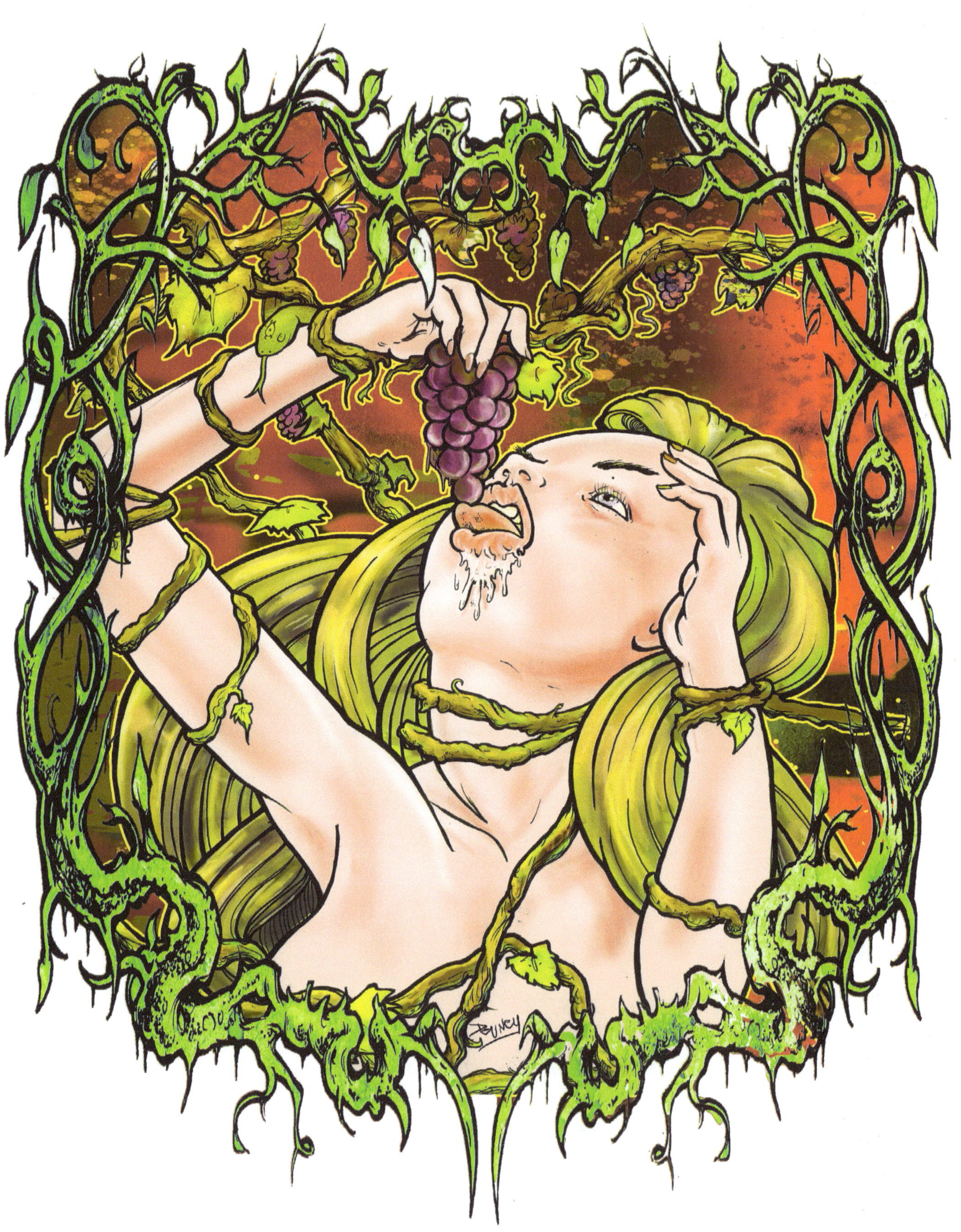

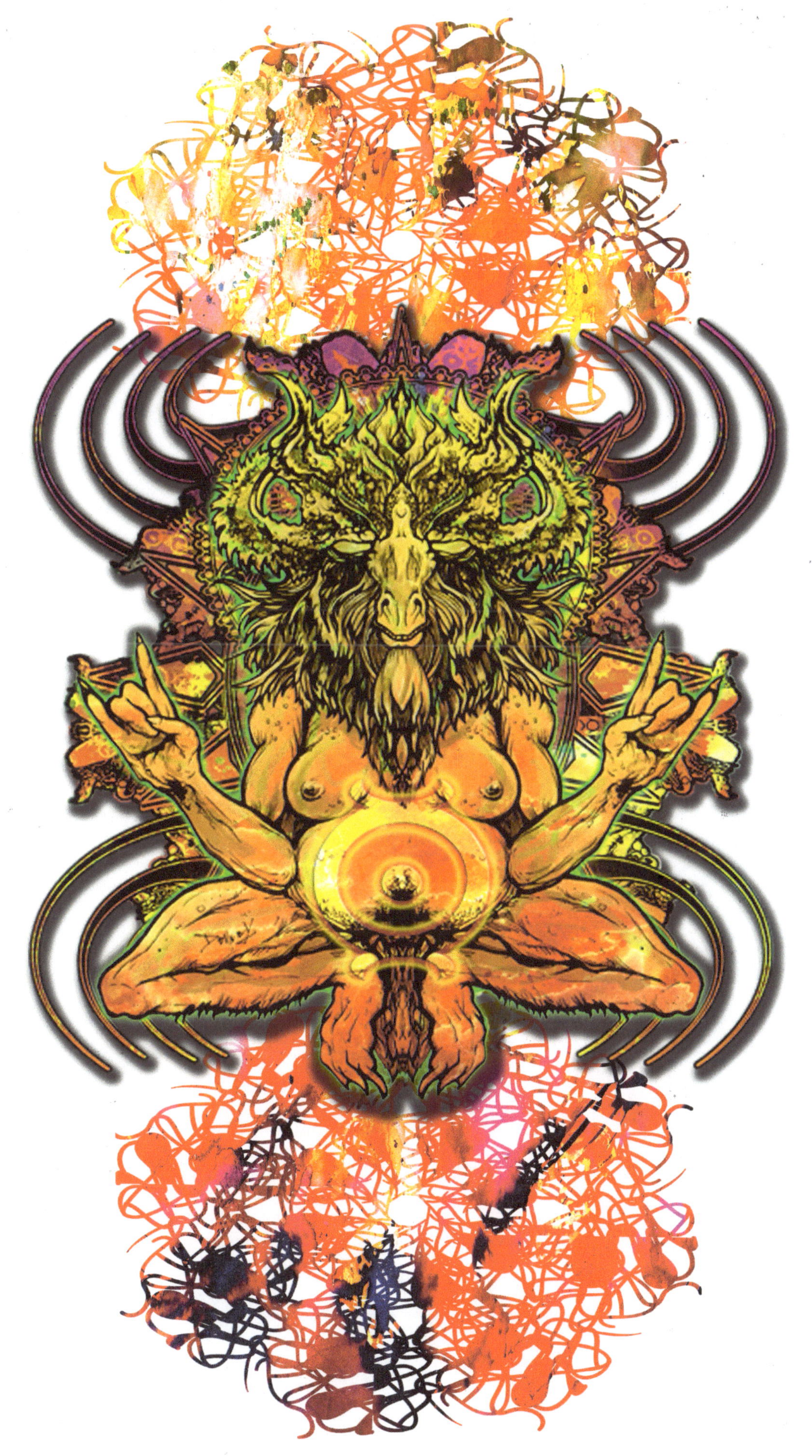

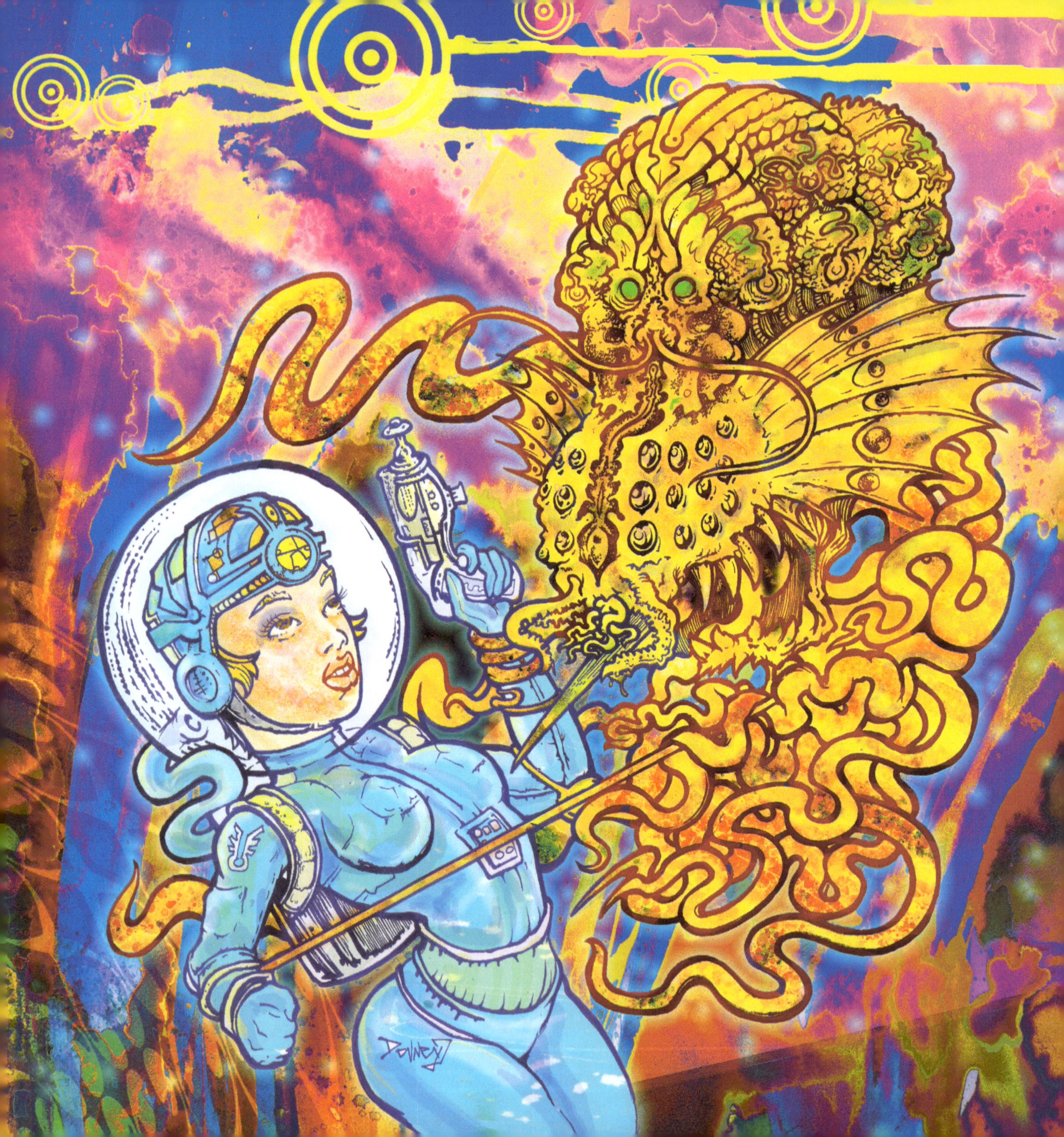
Downey

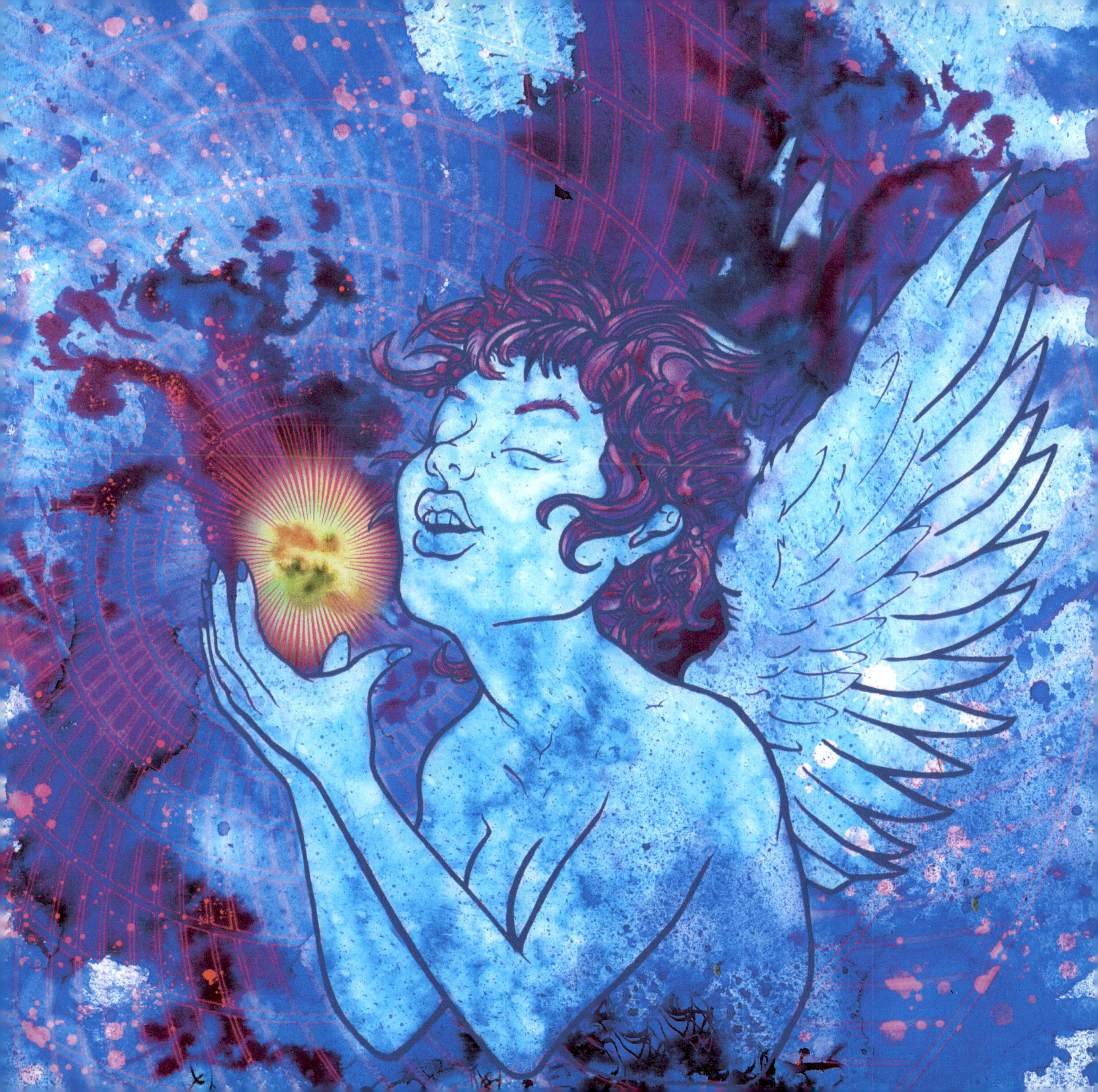

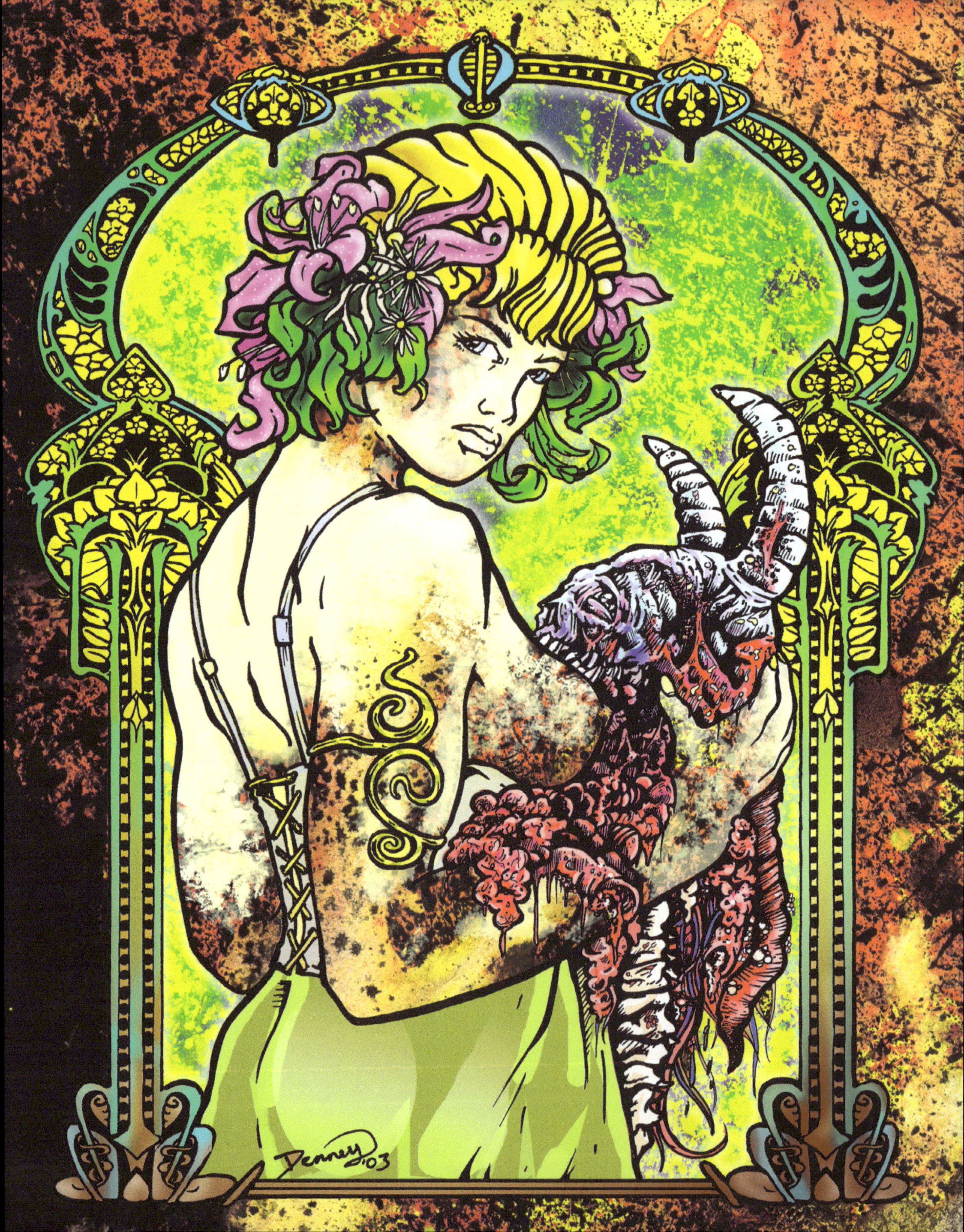
Denney '03

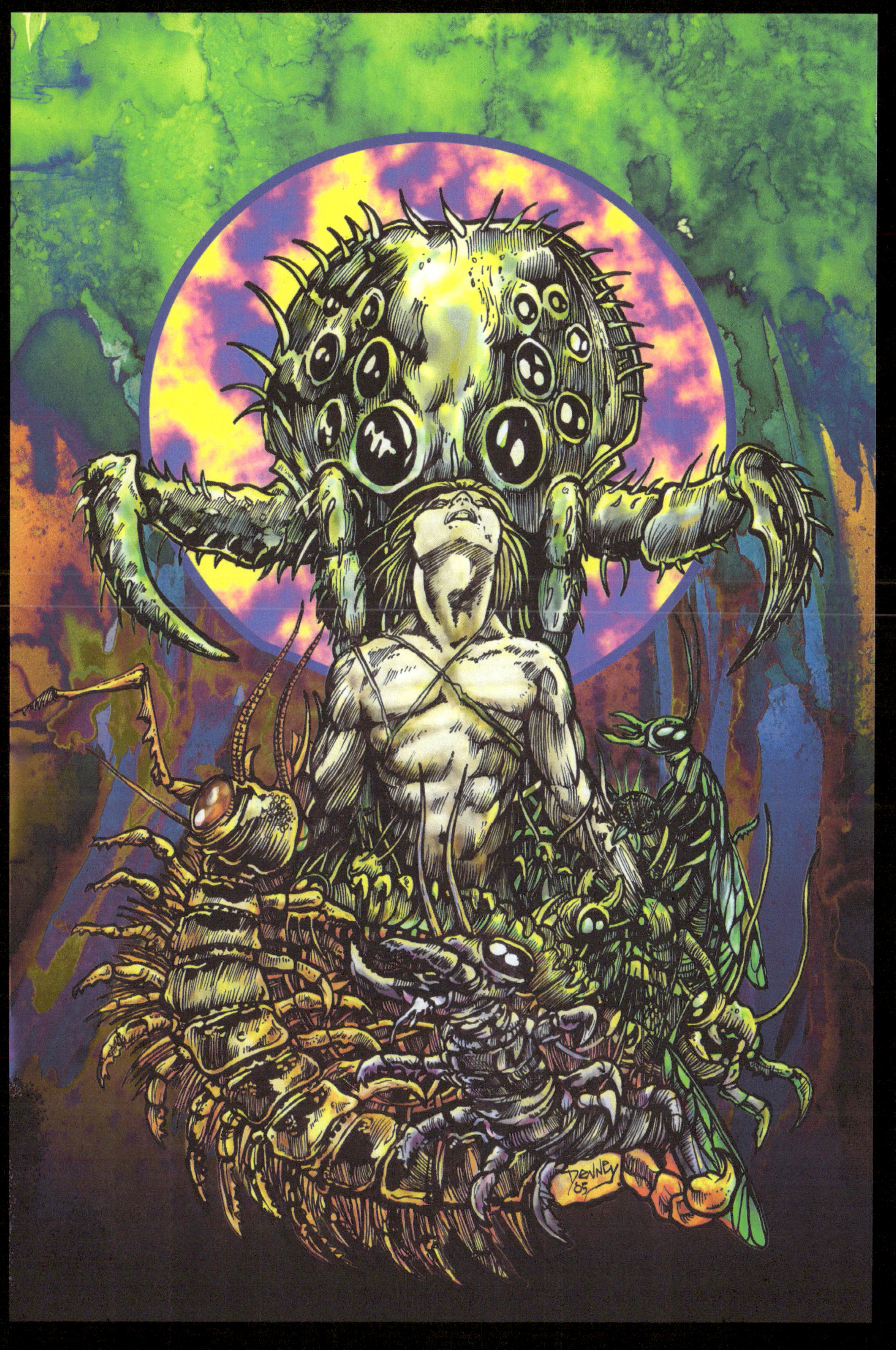
Denney '05

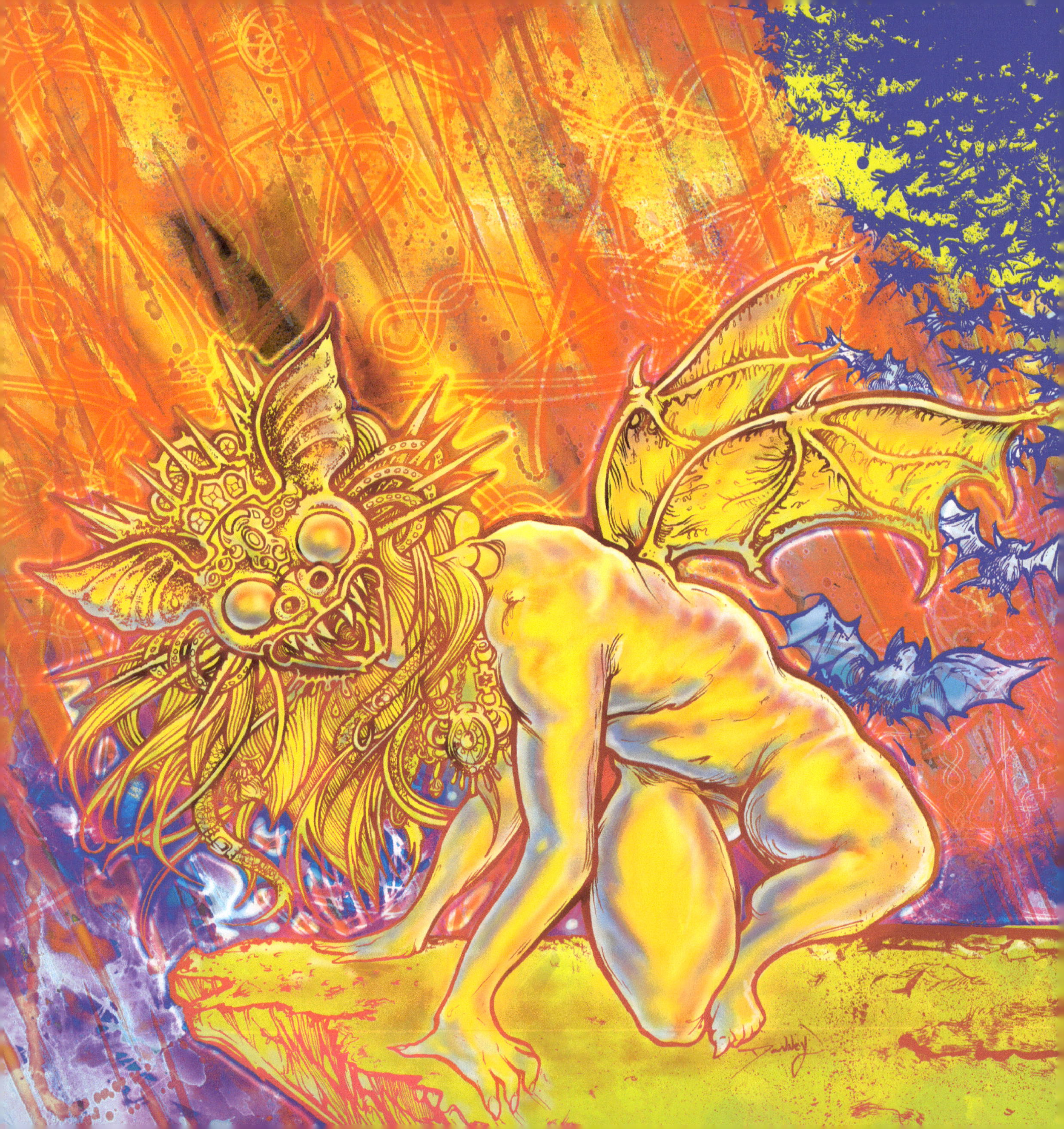

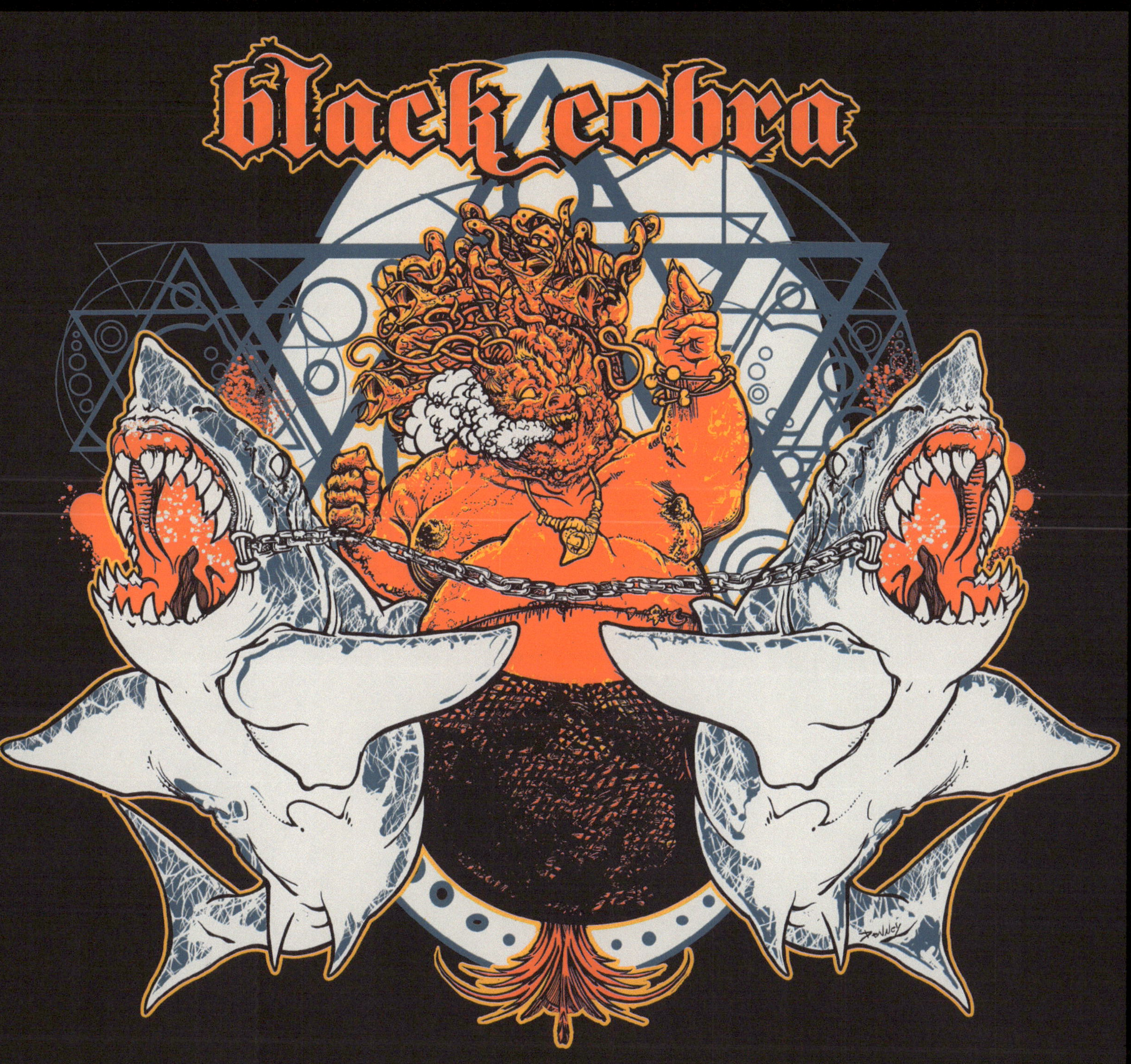
black cobra

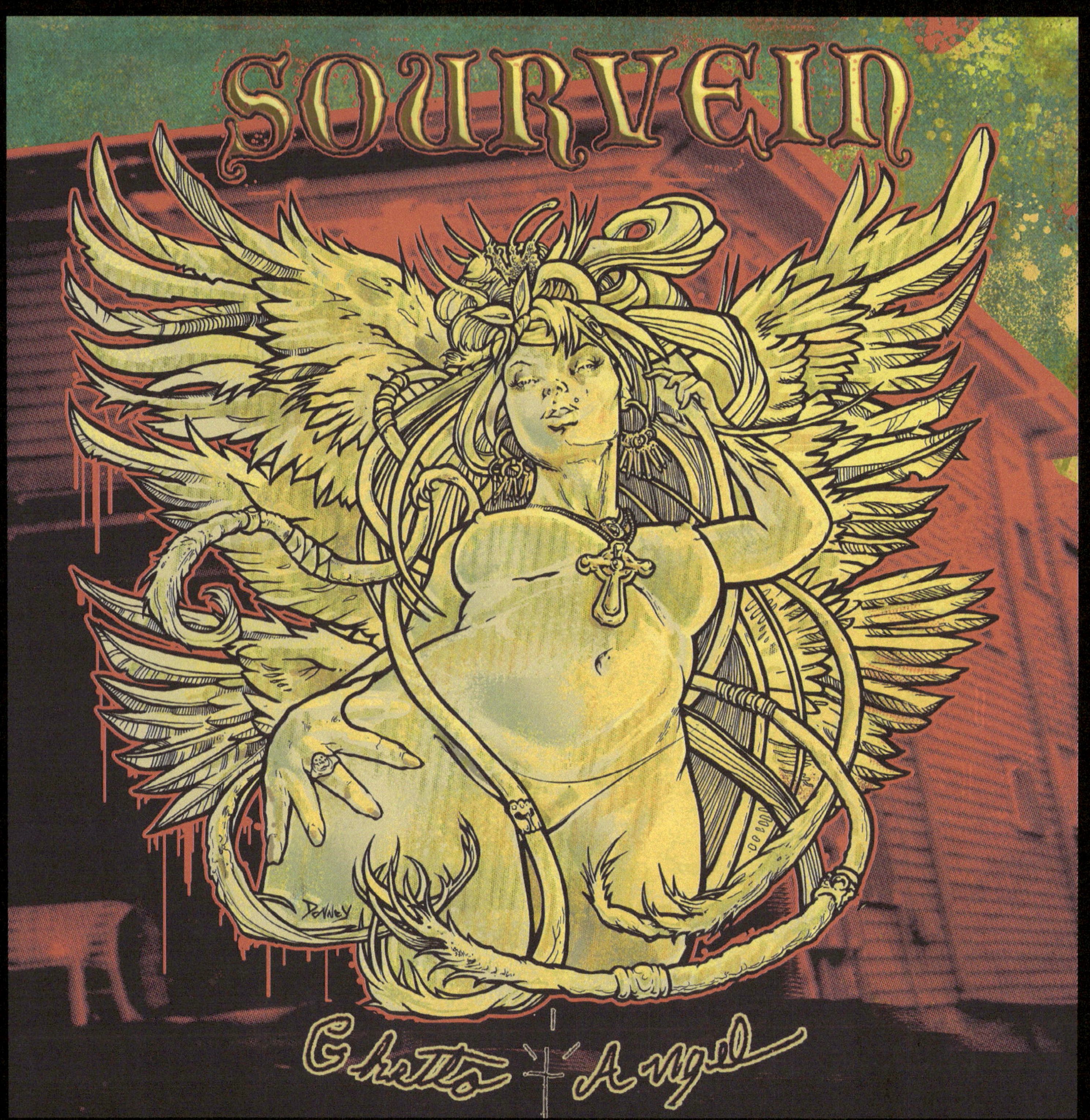
SOURVEIN
Ghetto Angel
Donney

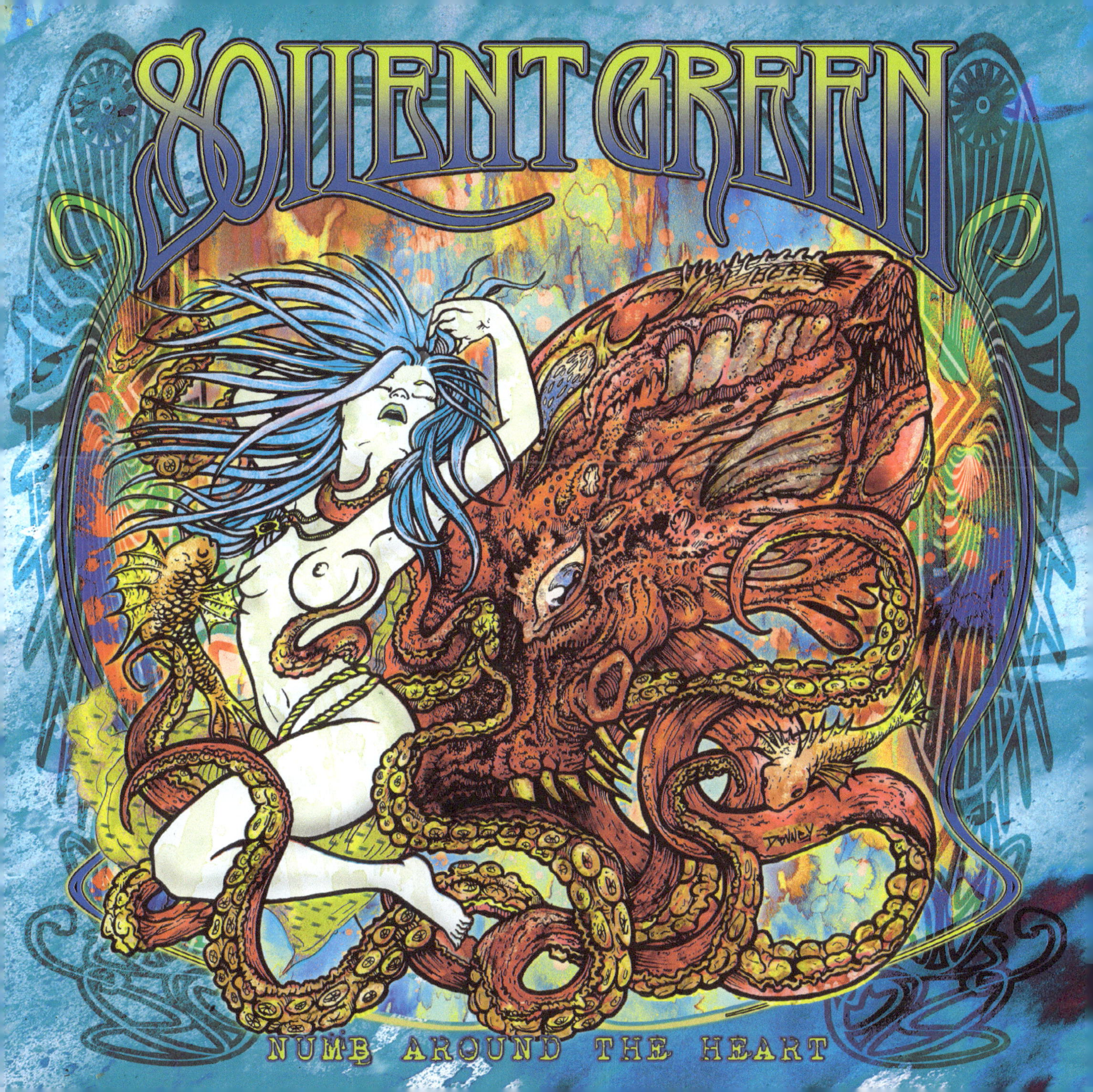
SOILENT GREEN
NUMB AROUND THE HEART

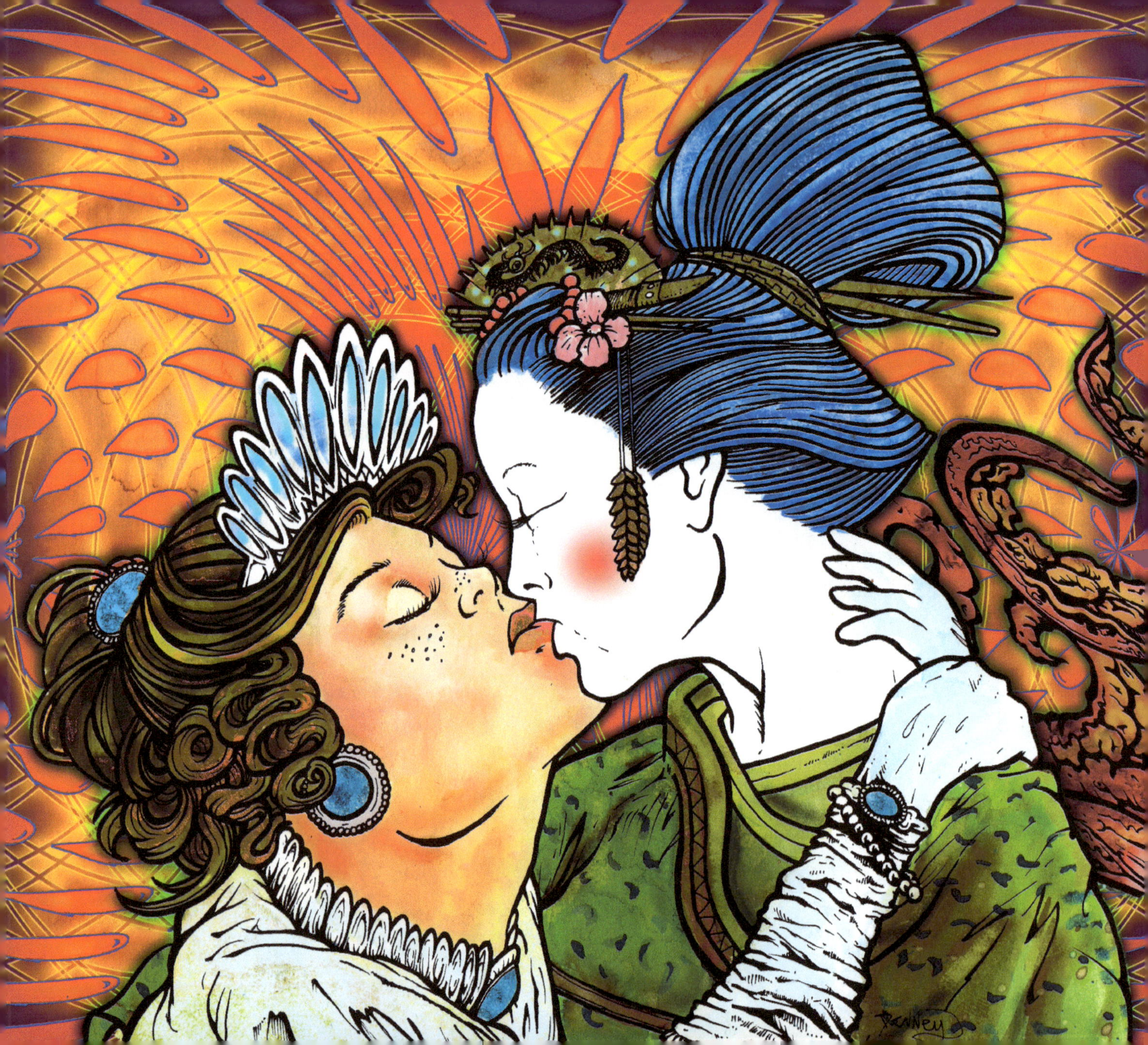

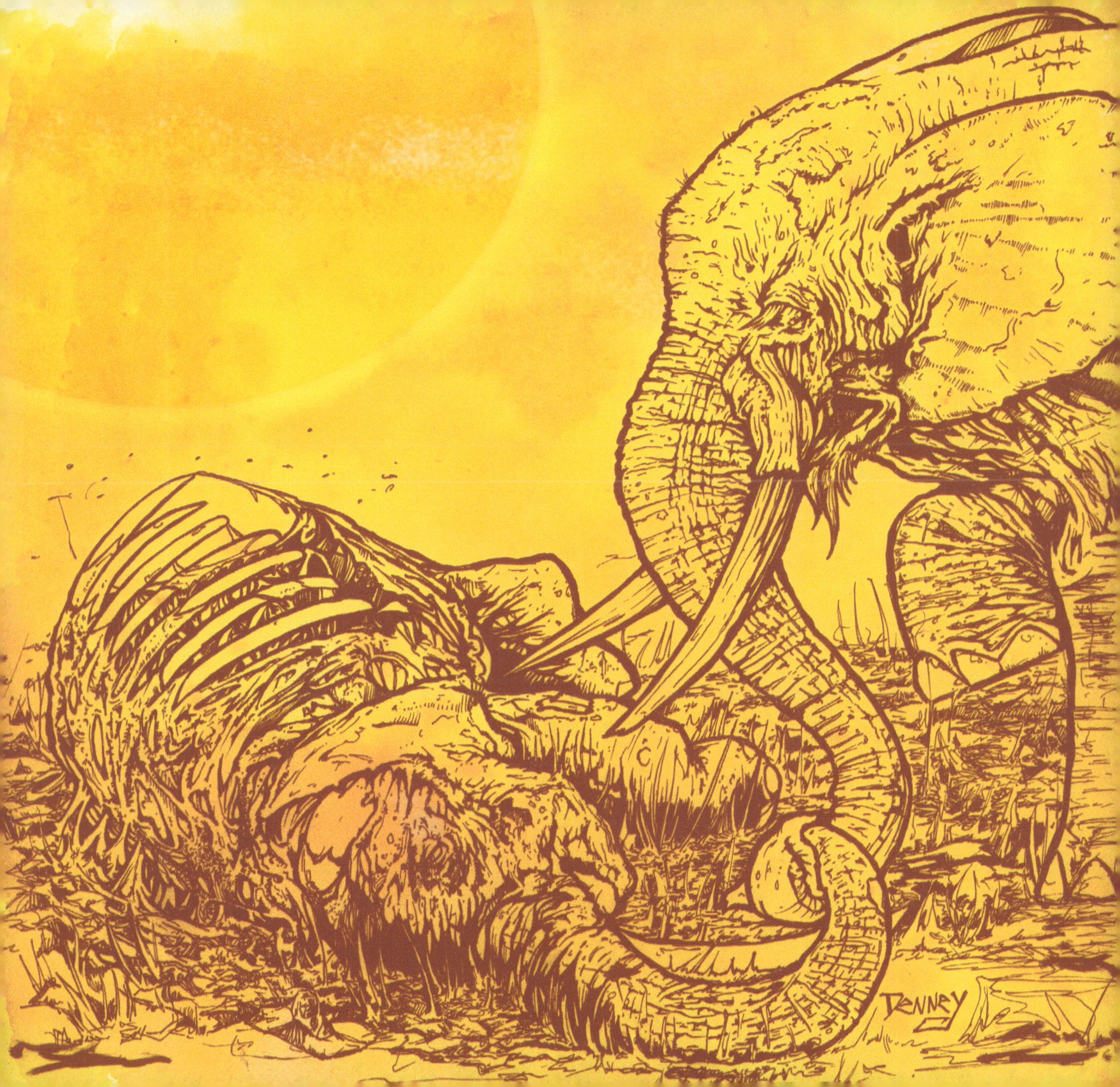
DENNEY

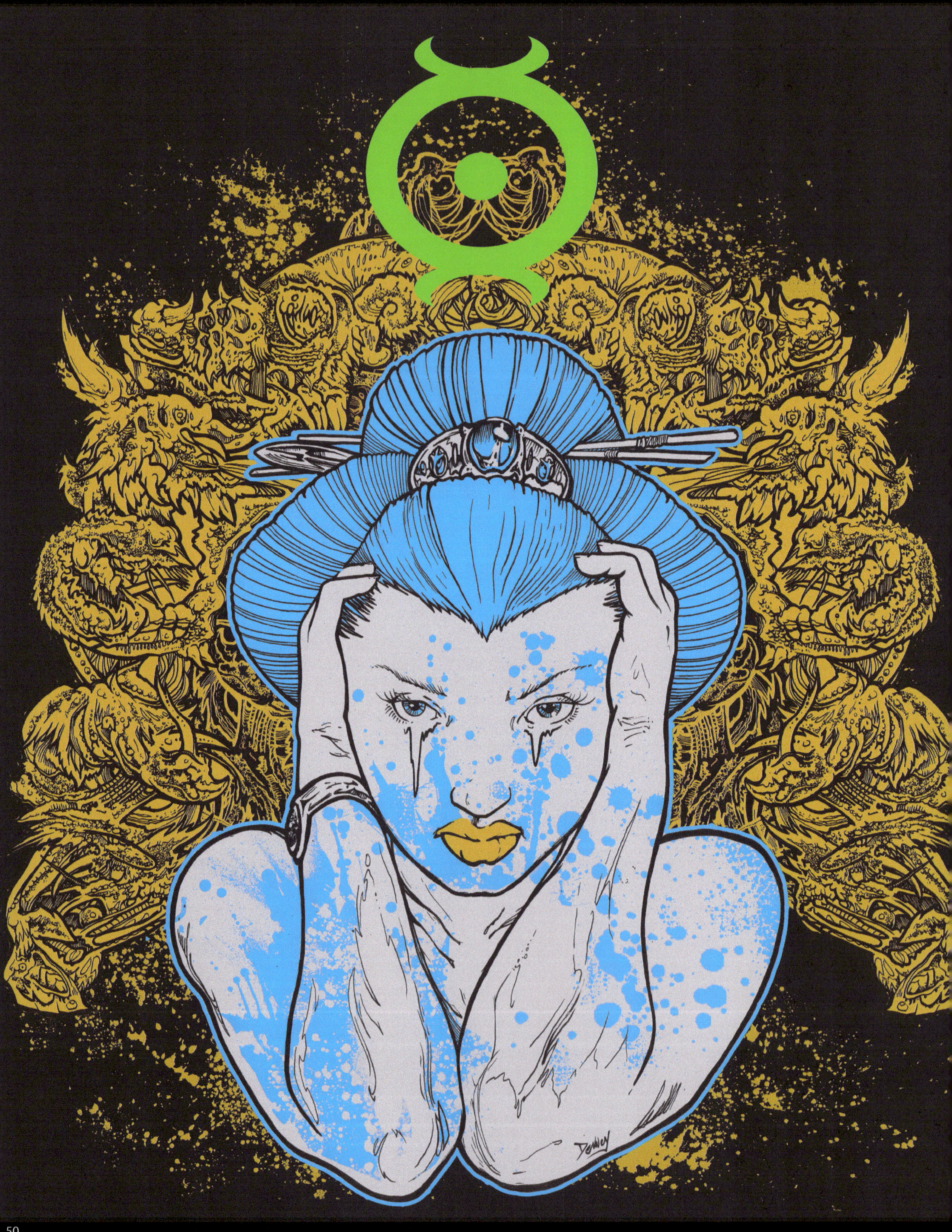

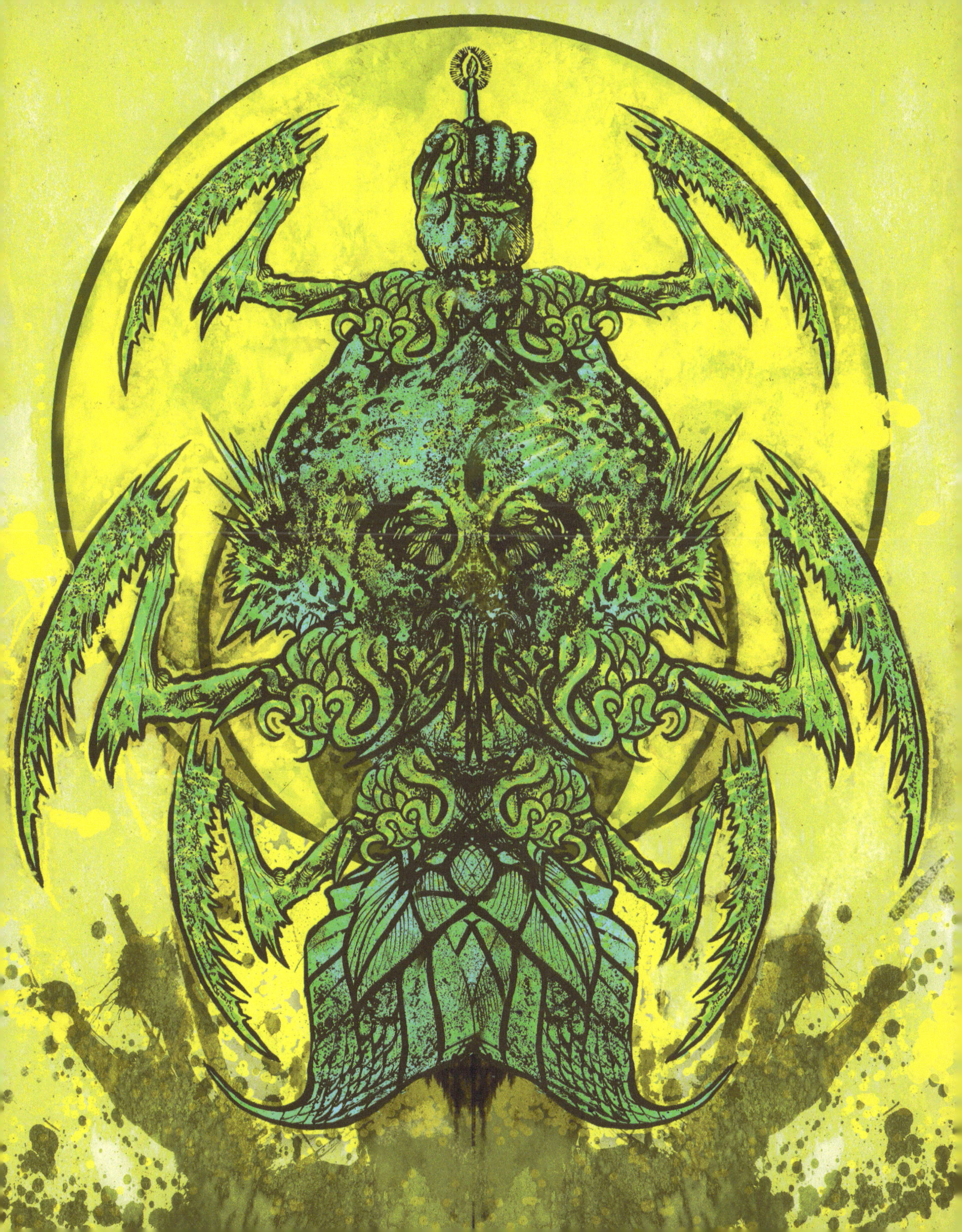

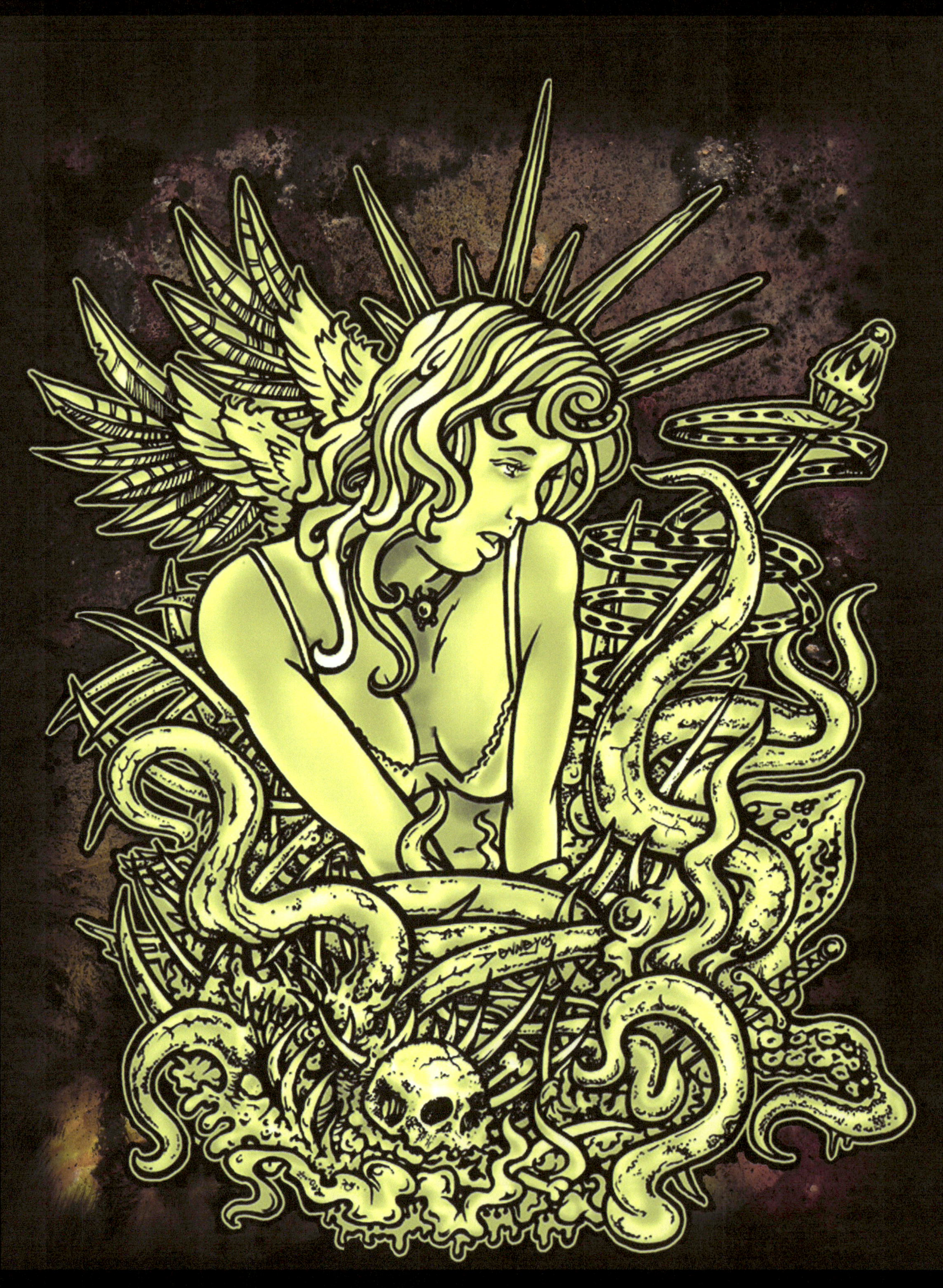

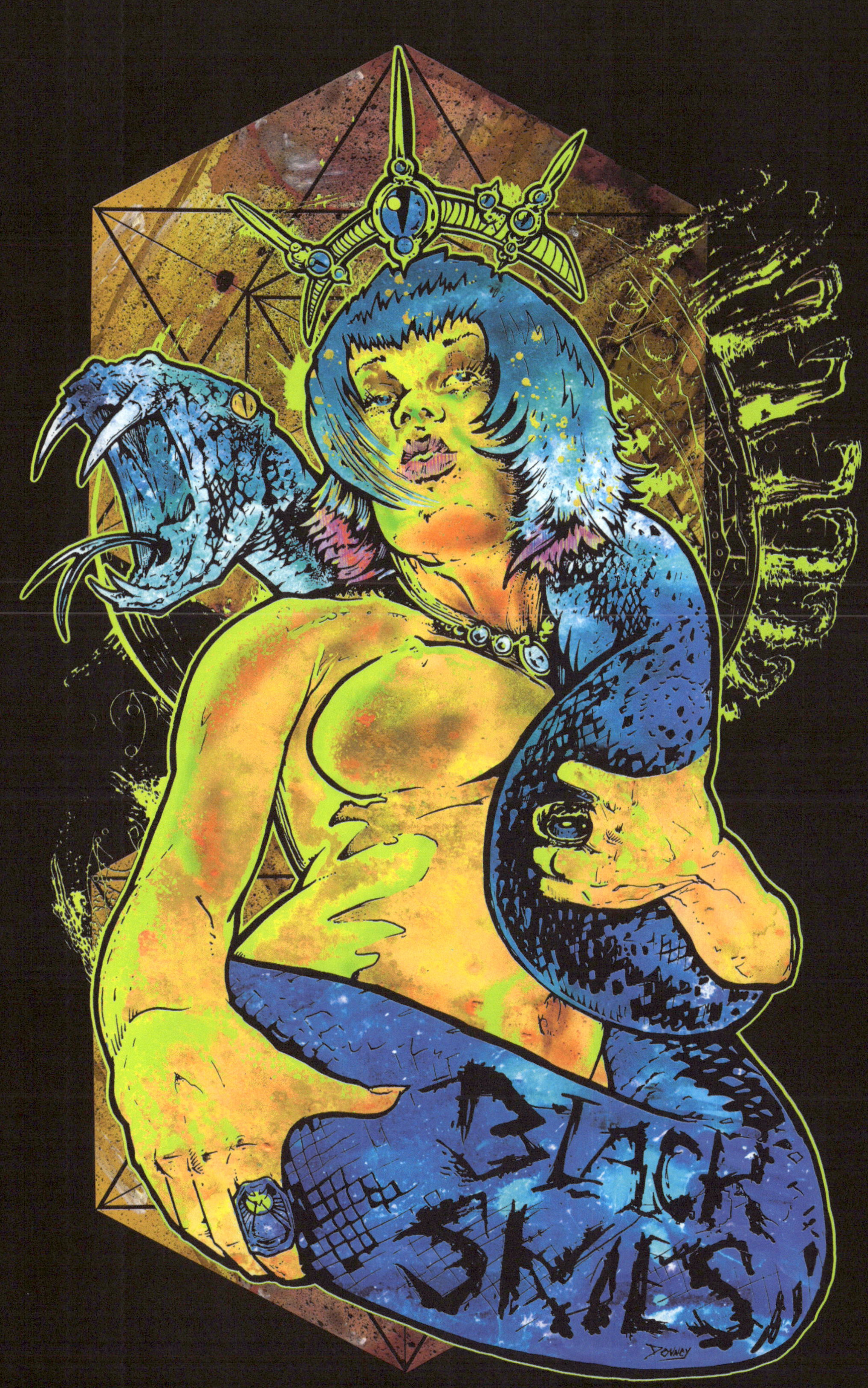
BLACK
SKULLS

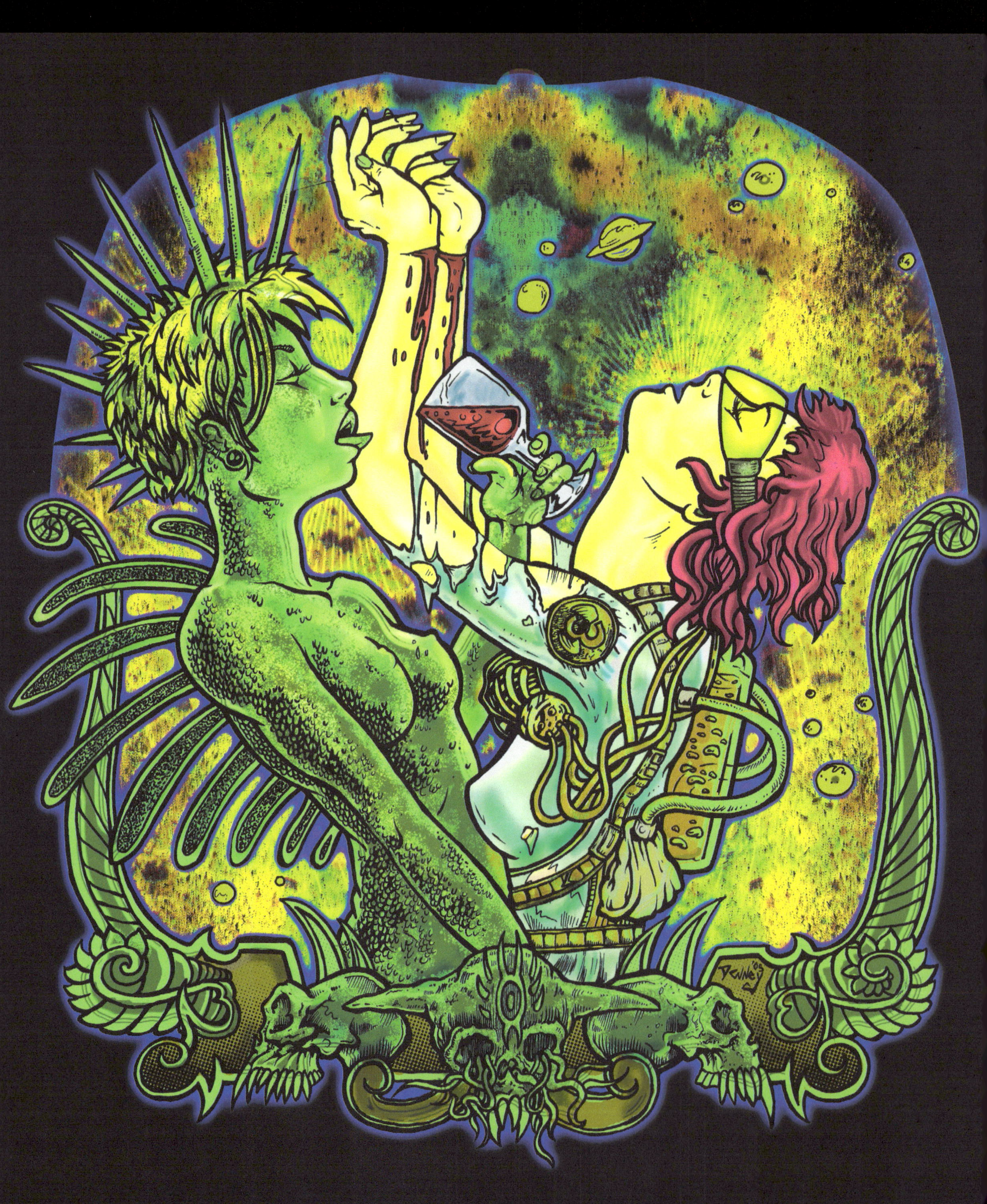

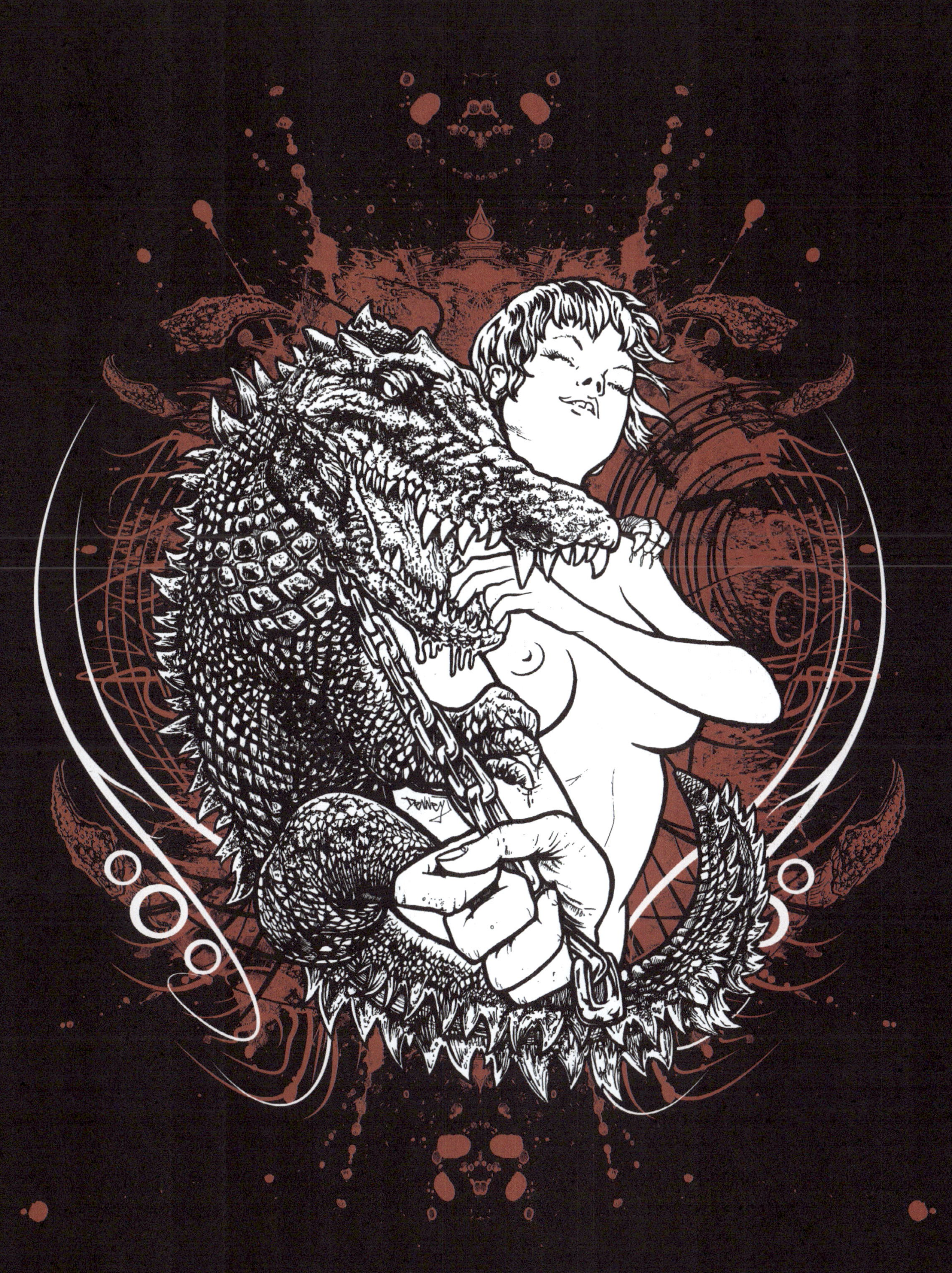

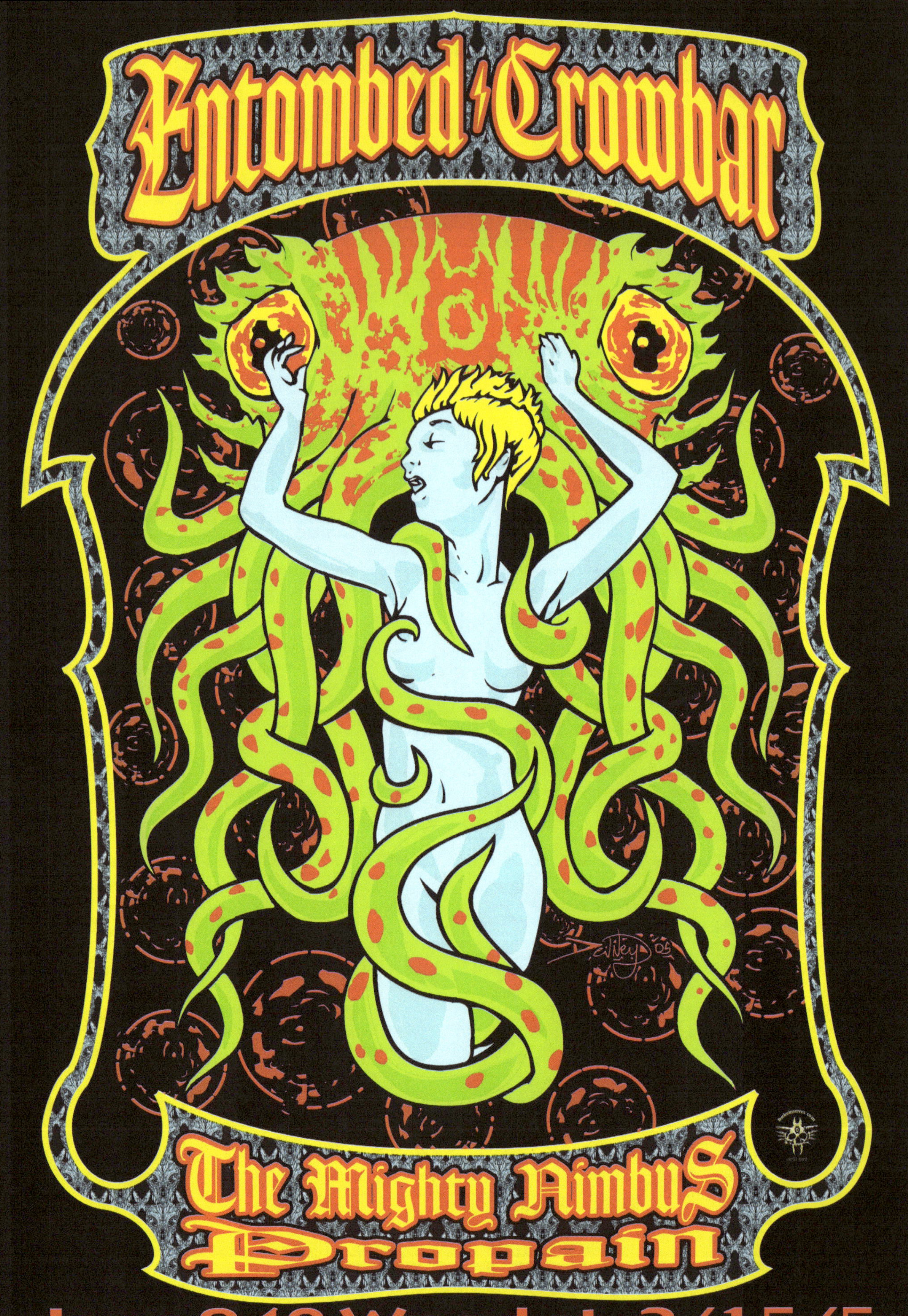
Entombed Crowbar
The Mighty Nimbus
Propain
Joes 940 Weed st. 2/15/5

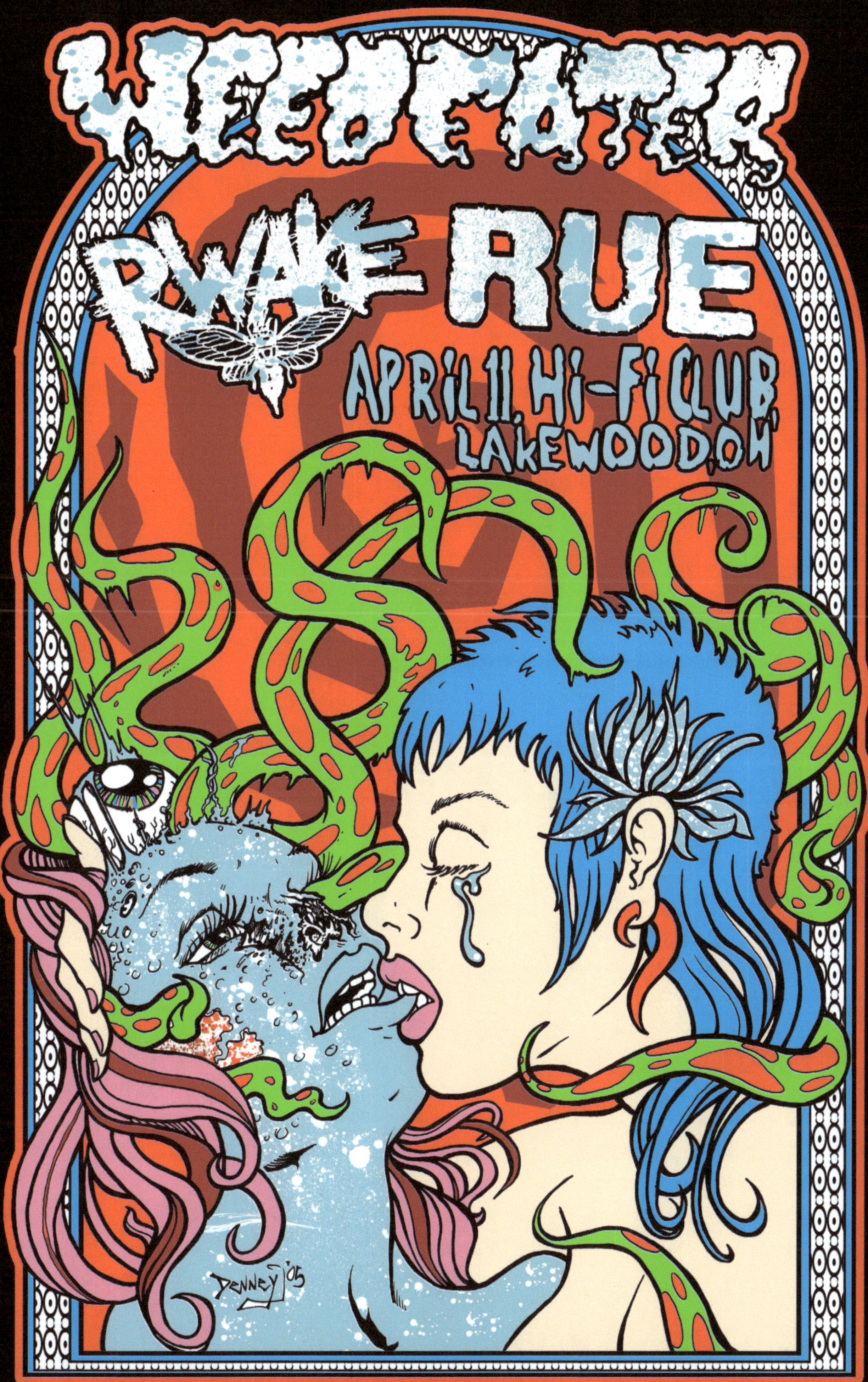
WEEDEATER
RWAKE
RUE
APRIL 11, HI-FI CLUB,
LAKEWOOD, OH
DENNEY '05

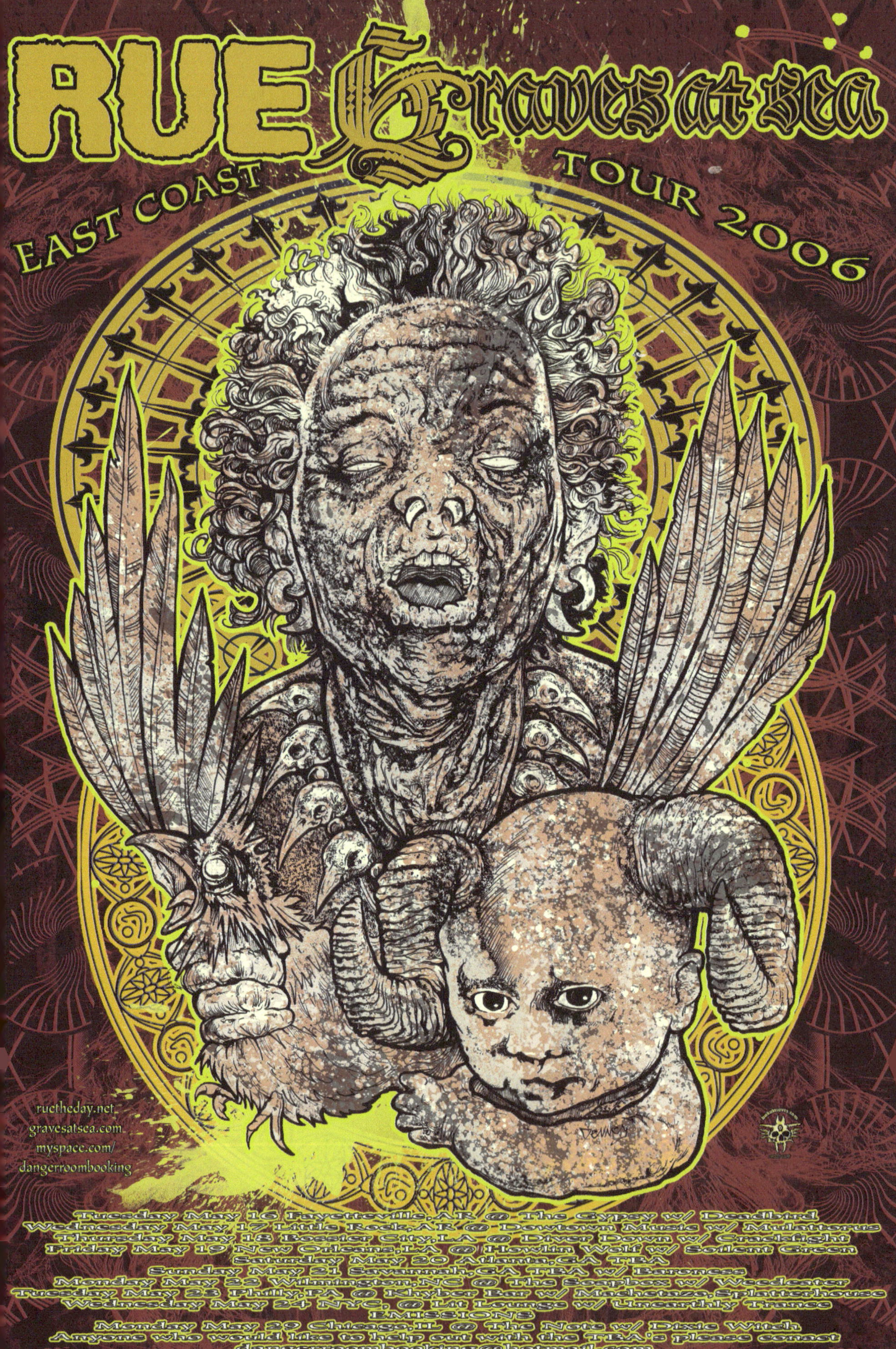
RUE
Graves at Sea
EAST COAST
TOUR 2006
ruetheday.net
gravesatsea.com
myspace.com/
dangerroombooking
Tuesday May 16 Fayetteville,AR @ The Gypsy w/ Deadbird
Wednesday May 17 Little Rock,AR @ Dowtown Music w/ Mulattorus
Thursday May 18 Bossier City,LA @ Diver Down w/ Crackfight
Friday May 19 New Orleans,LA @ Howlin Wolf w/ Soilent Green
Saturday May 20 Atlanta,GA TBA
Sunday May 21 Savannah,GA TBA w/ Baroness
Monday May 22 Wilmington,NC @ The Soapbox w/ Weedeater
Tuesday May 23 Philly,PA @ Khyber Bar w/ Machetazo,Splatterhouse
Wednesday May 24 NYC, @ Lit Lounge w/ Unearthly Trance
EMISSIONS
Monday May 29 Chicago,IL @ The Note w/ Dixie Witch
Anyone who would like to help out with the TBA's please conact
dangerroombooking@hotmail.com

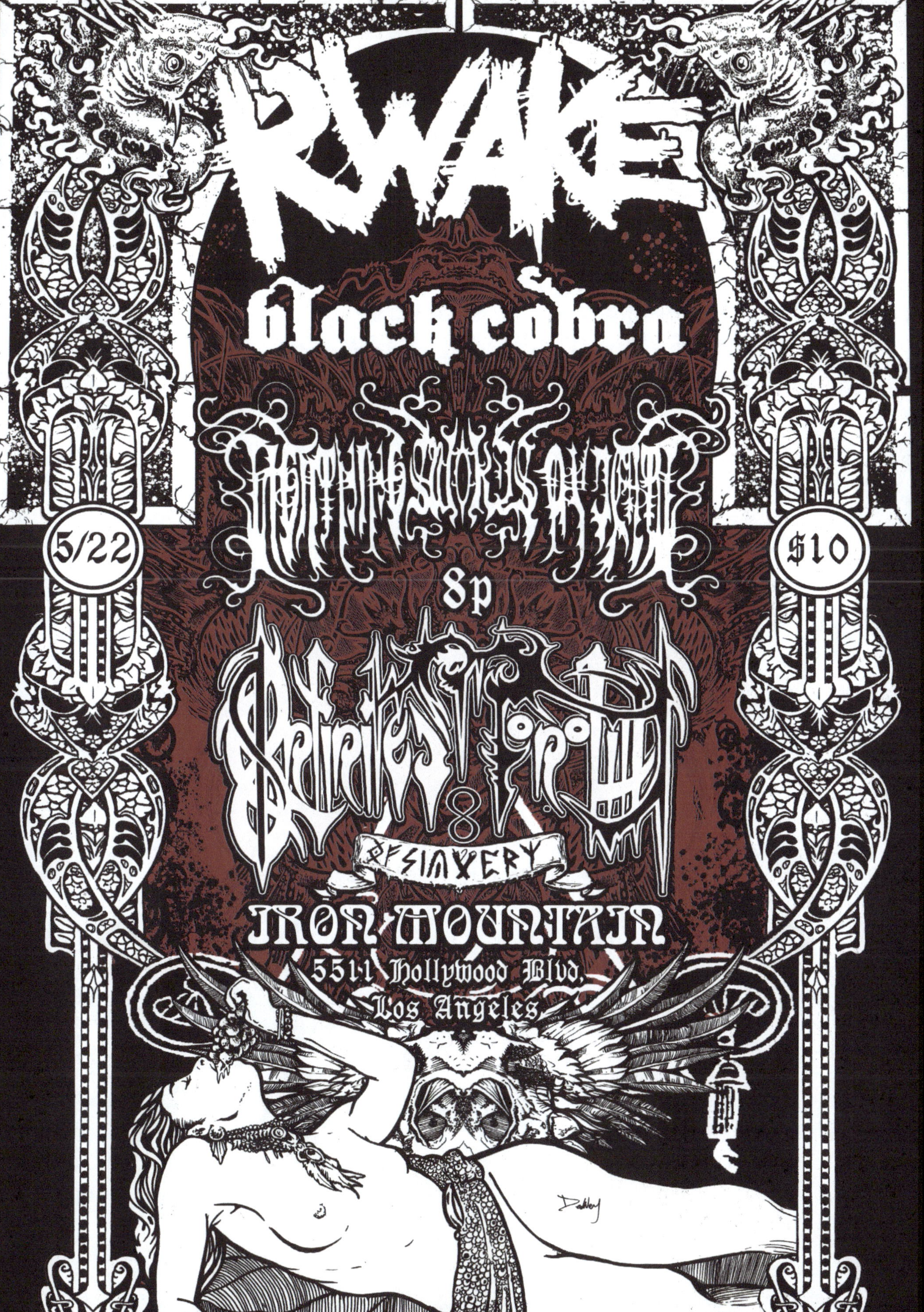
RWAKE
black cobra
5/22
$10
8p
IRON MOUNTAIN
5511 Hollywood Blvd.
Los Angeles

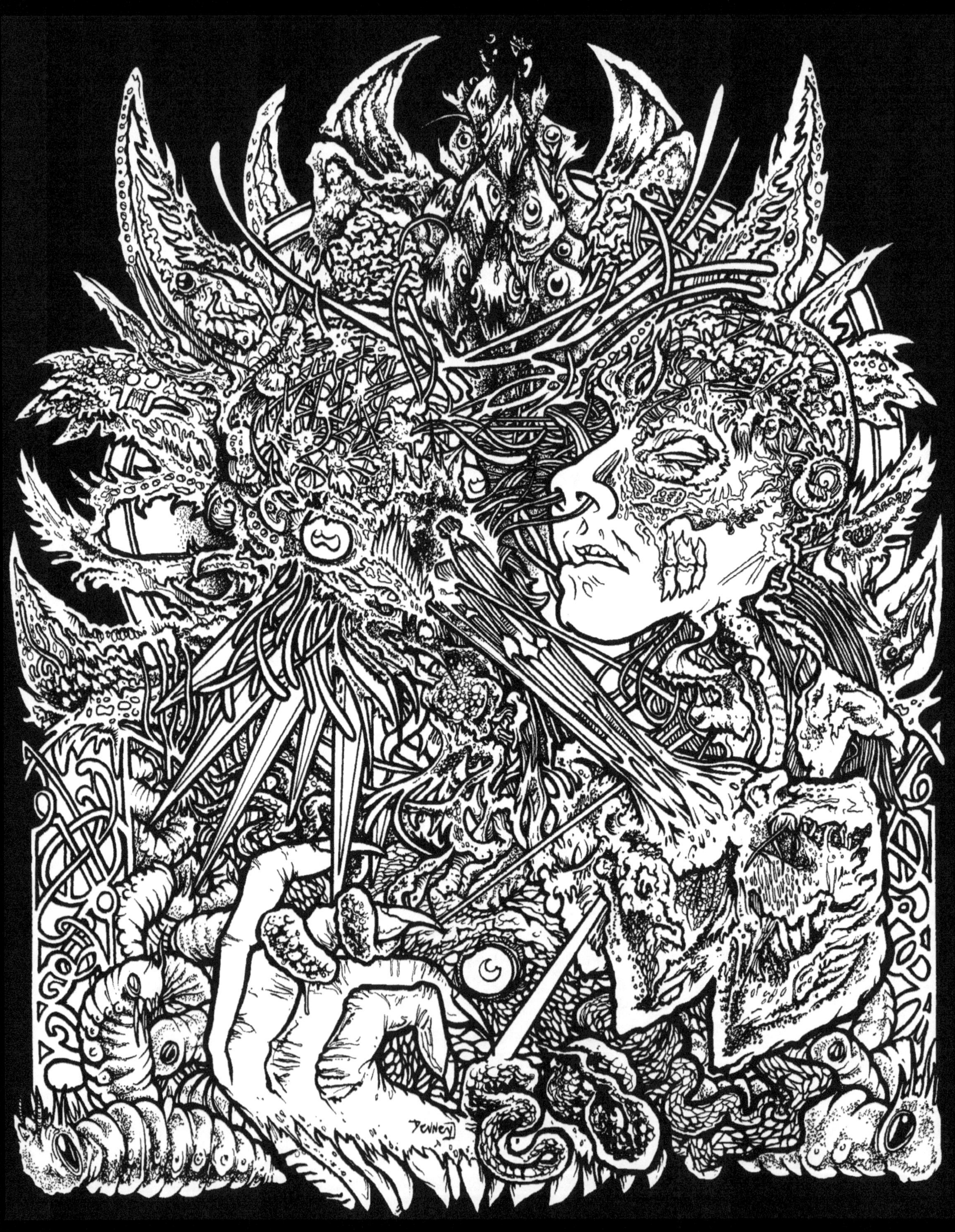
Denney

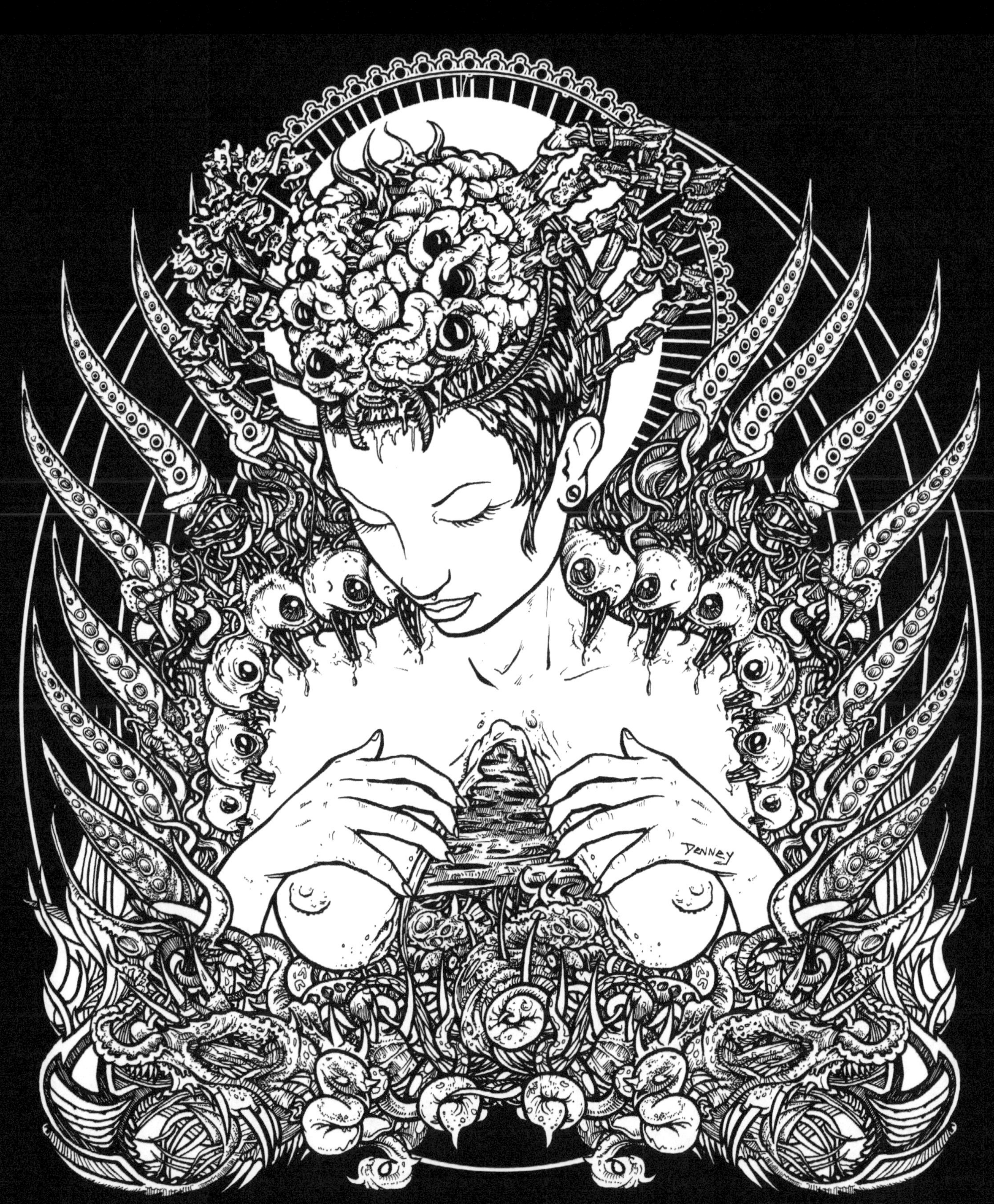
DENNEY

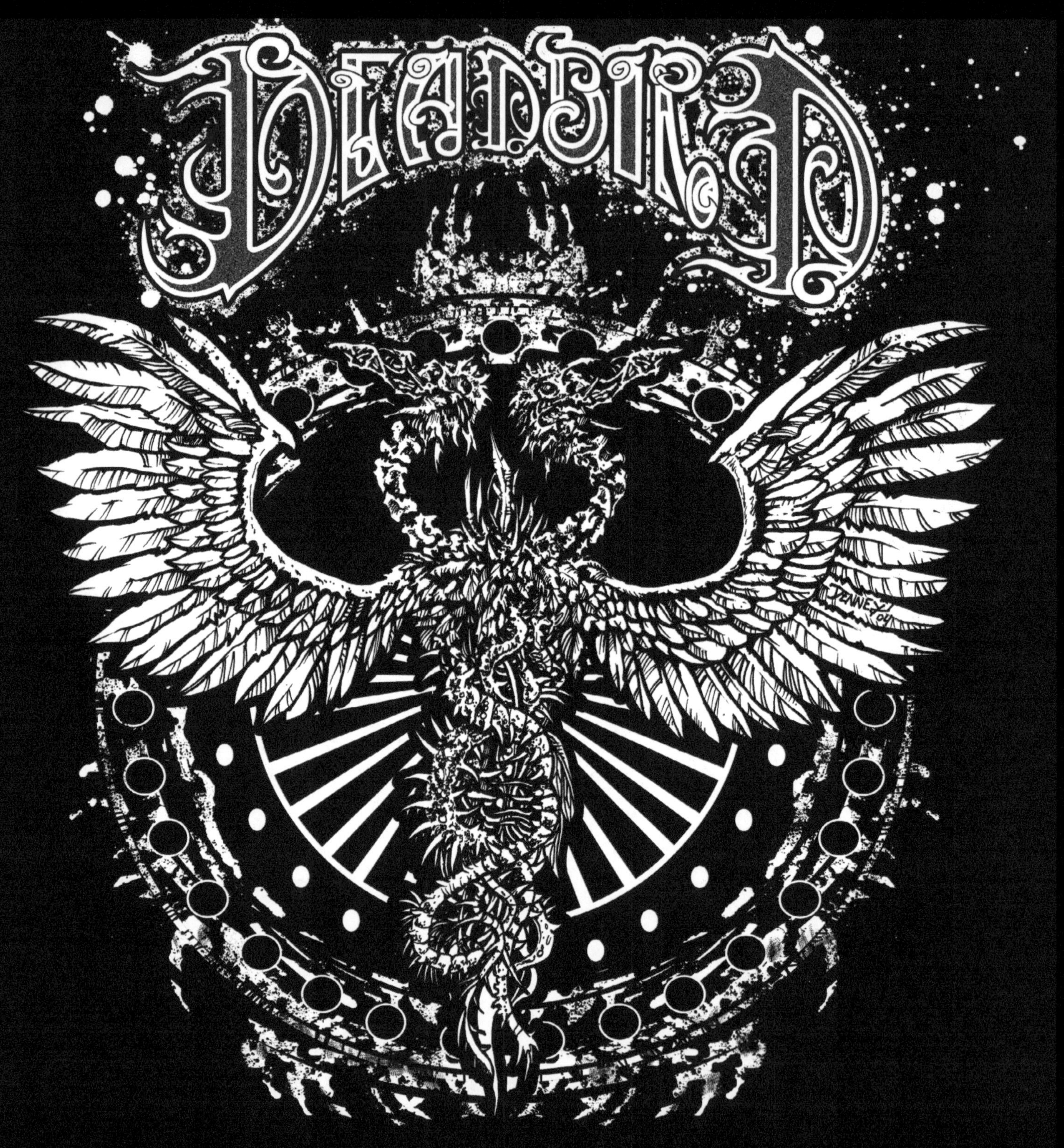
DEADBIRD

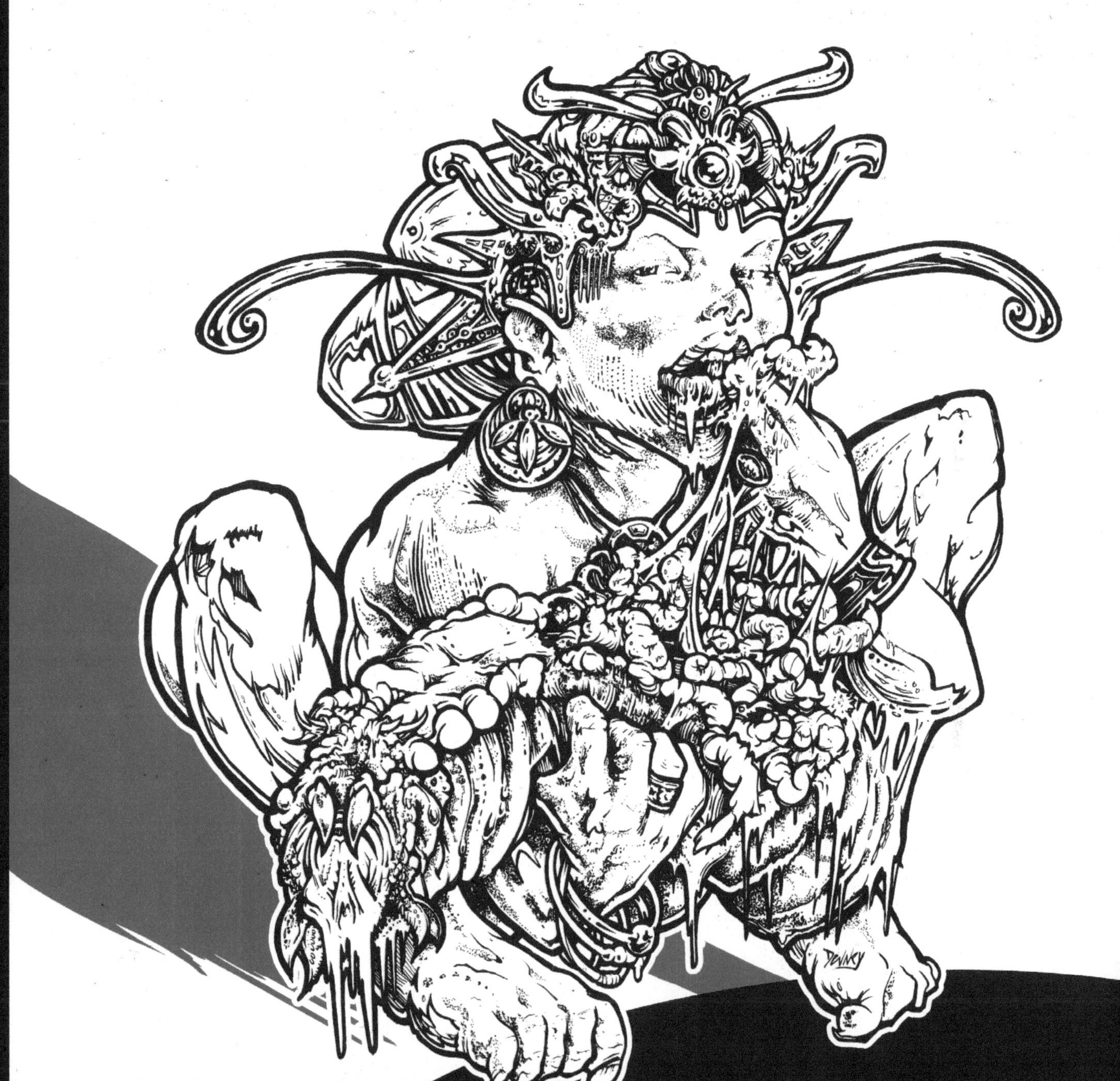

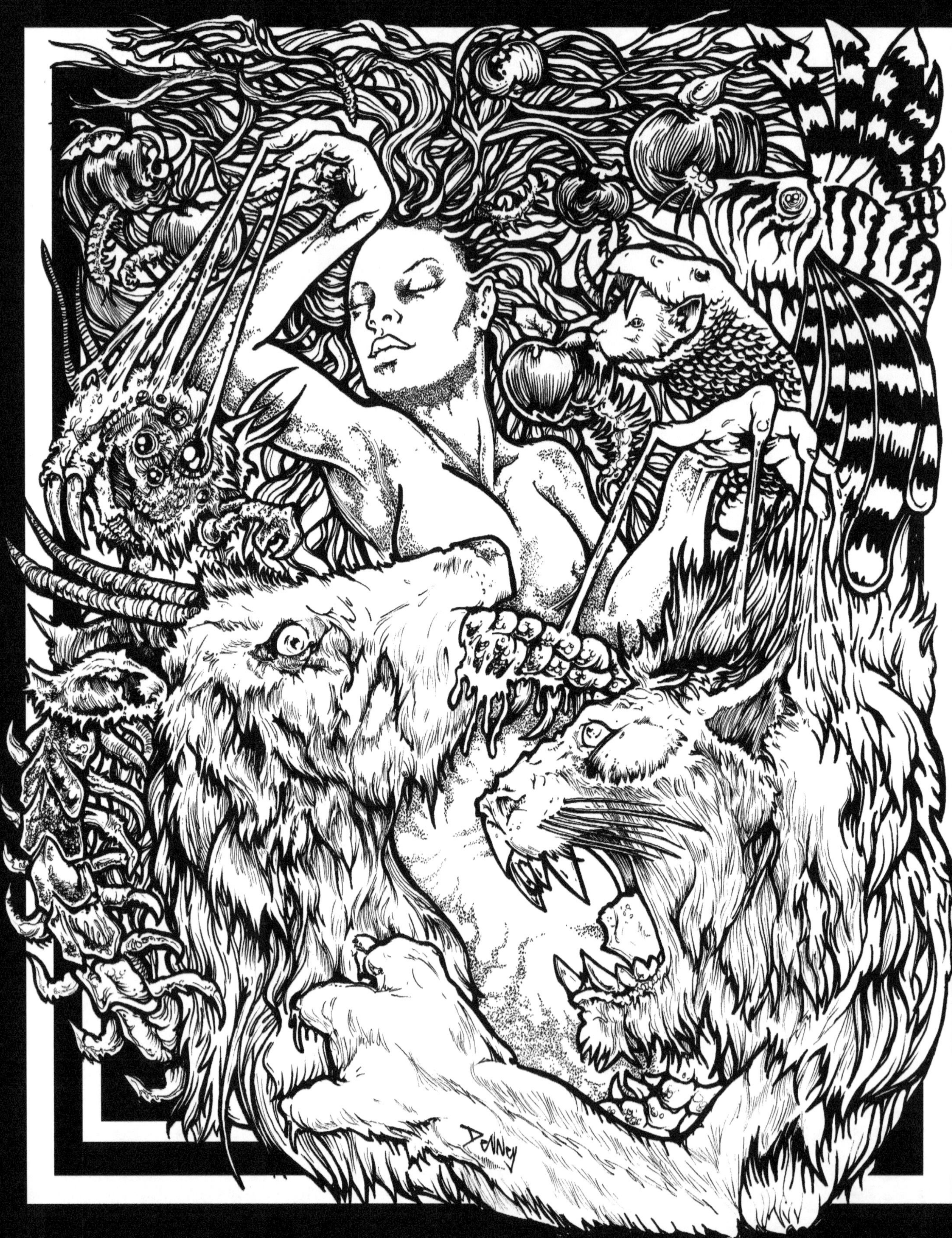
DeNNey

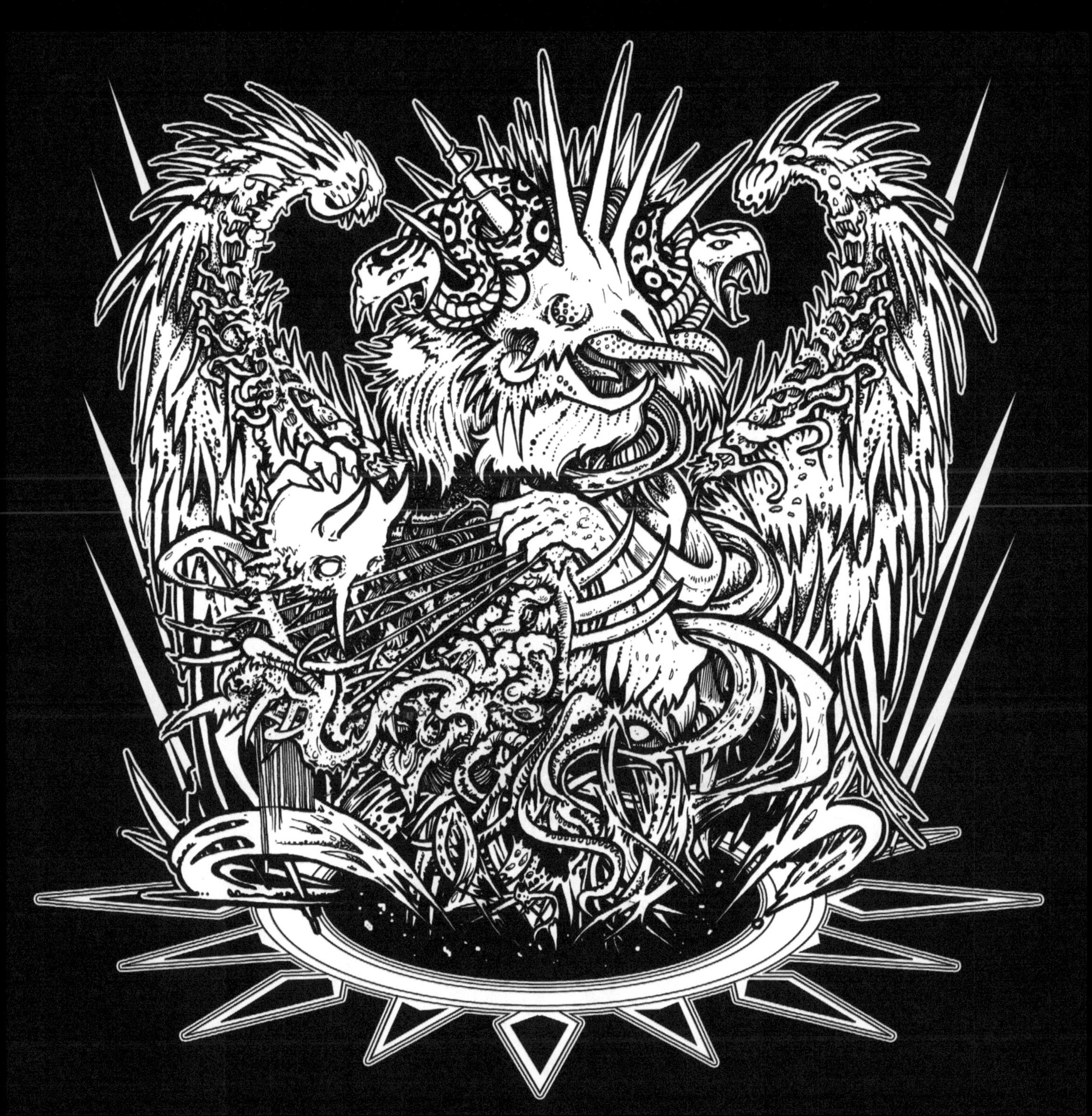

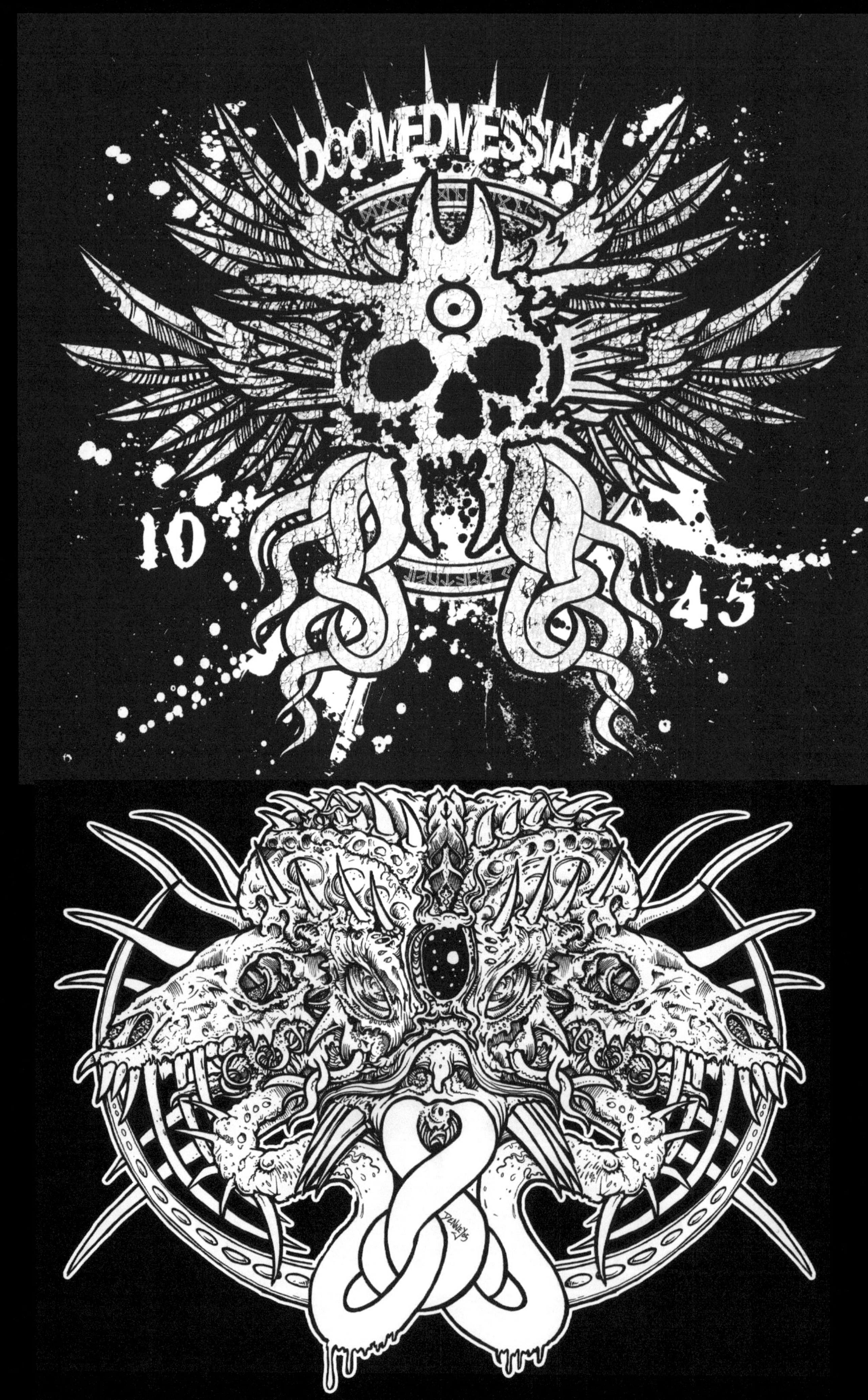
DOOMEDMESSIAH
10
45

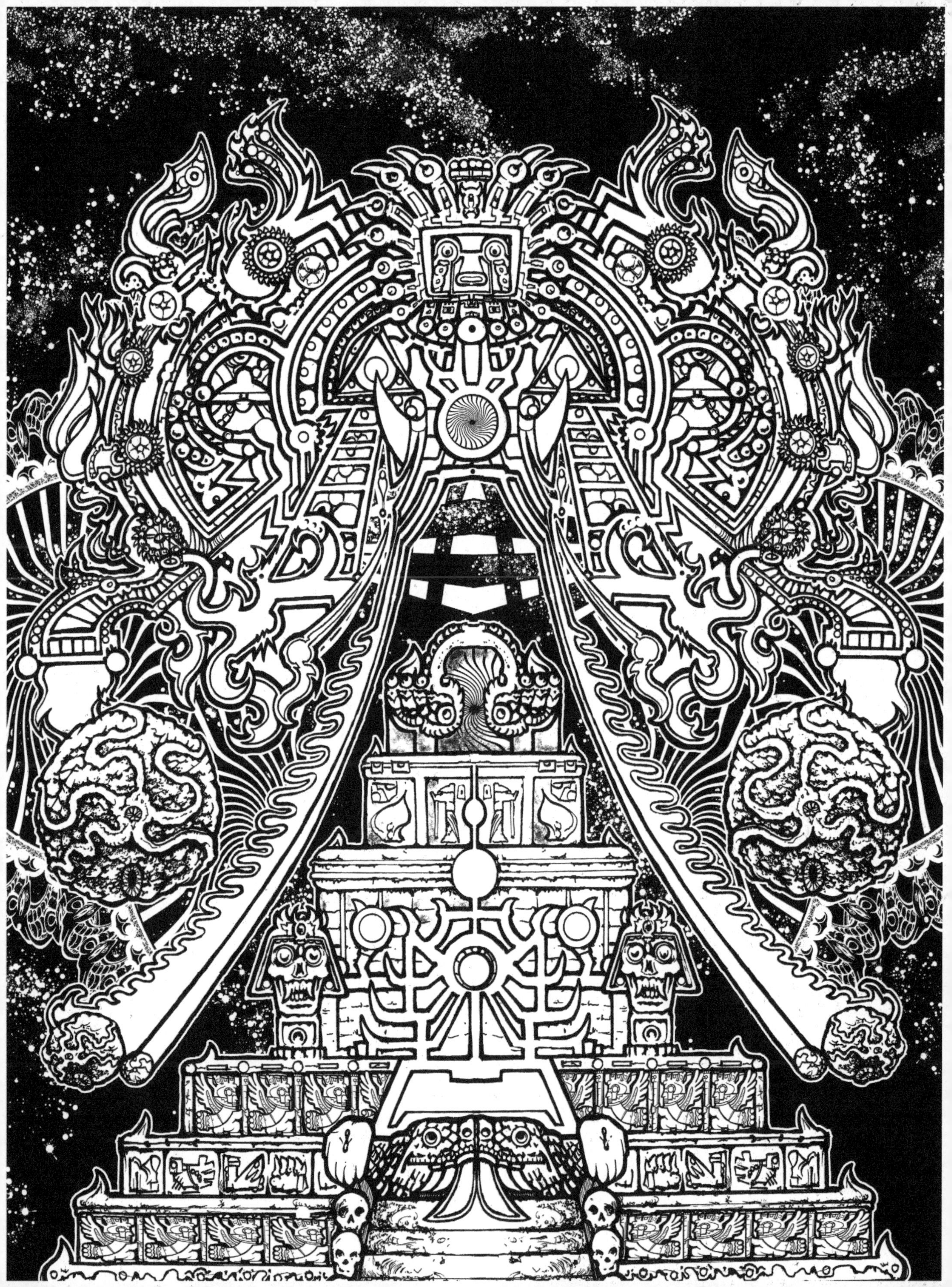

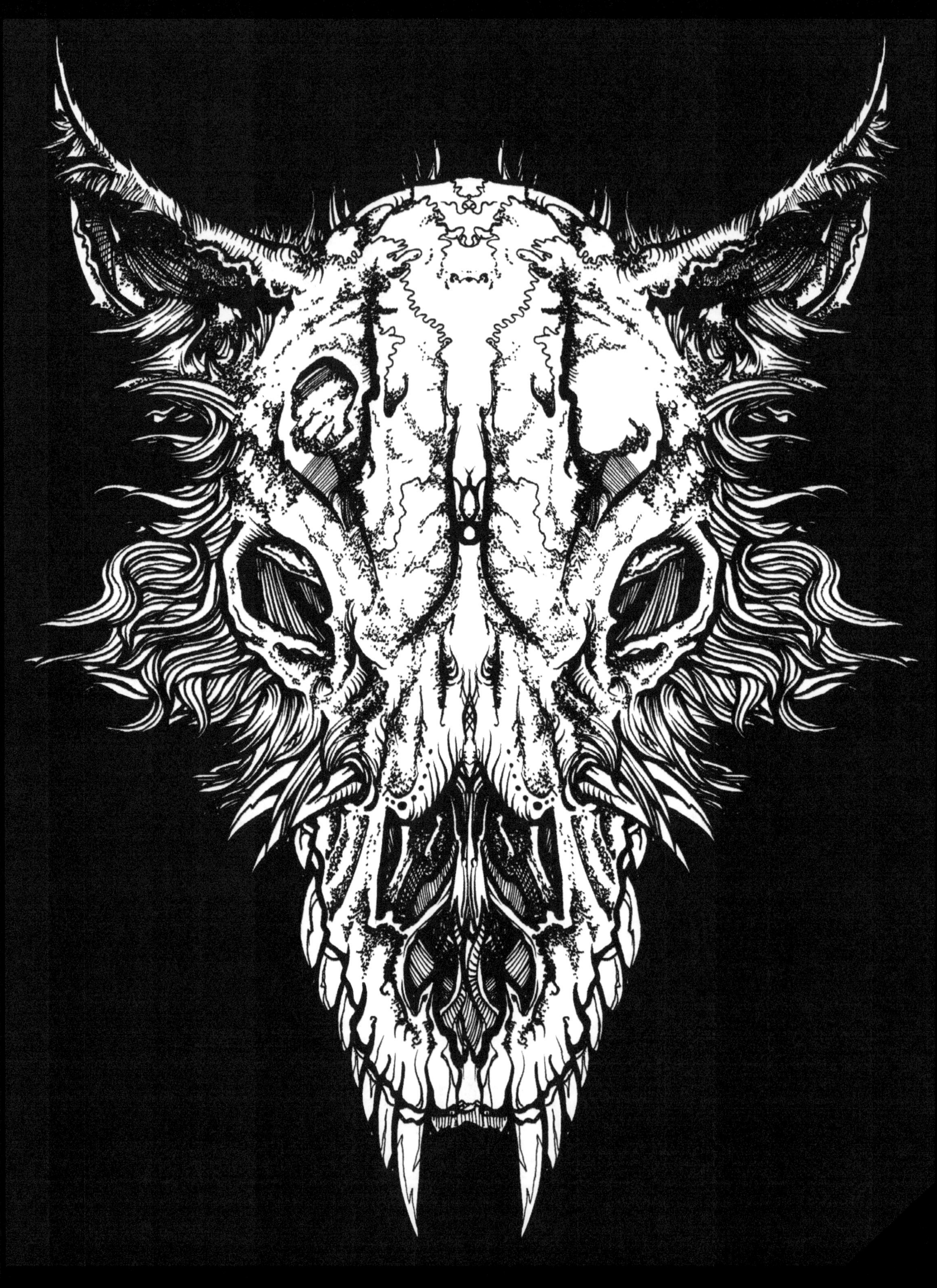

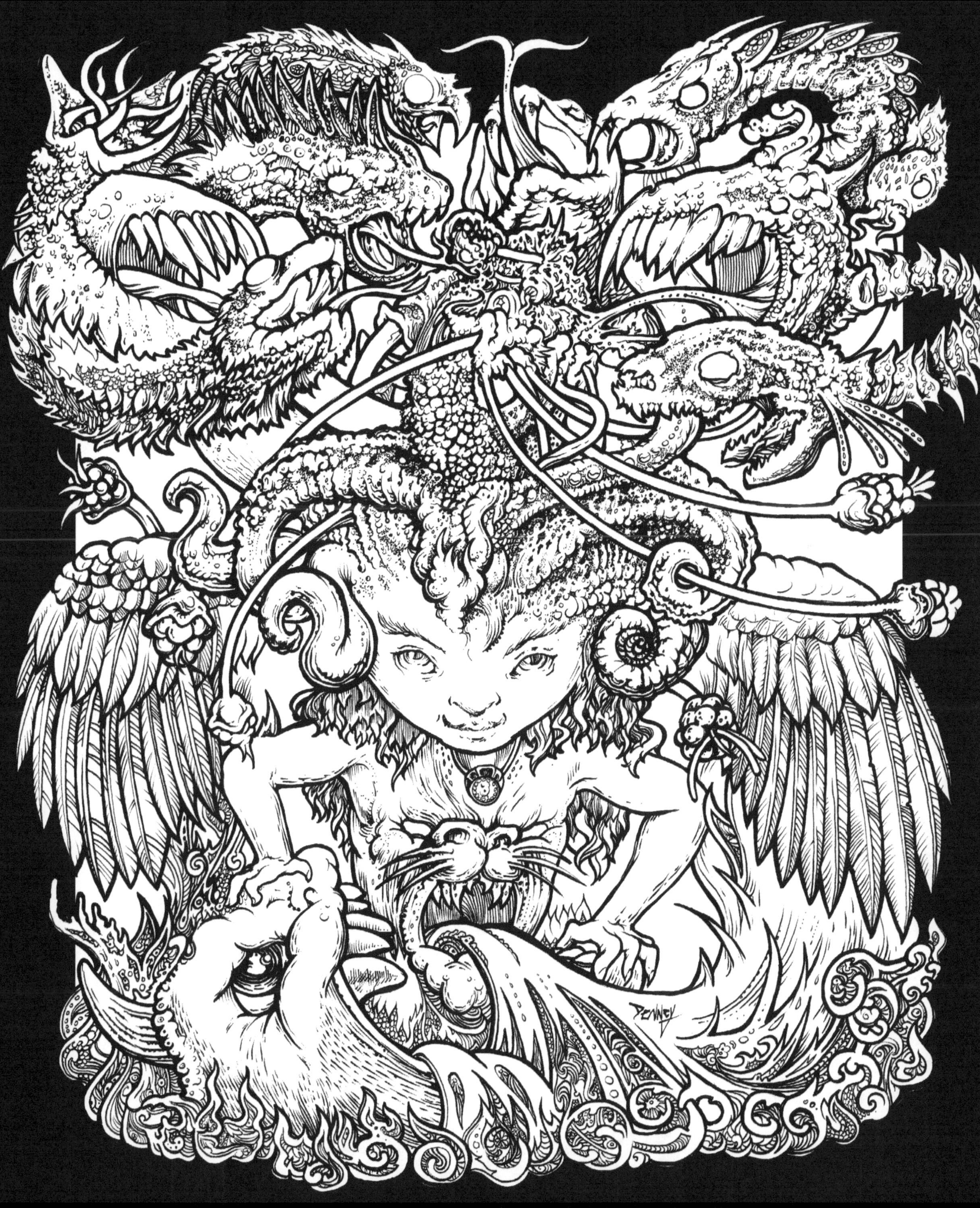
DENNEY

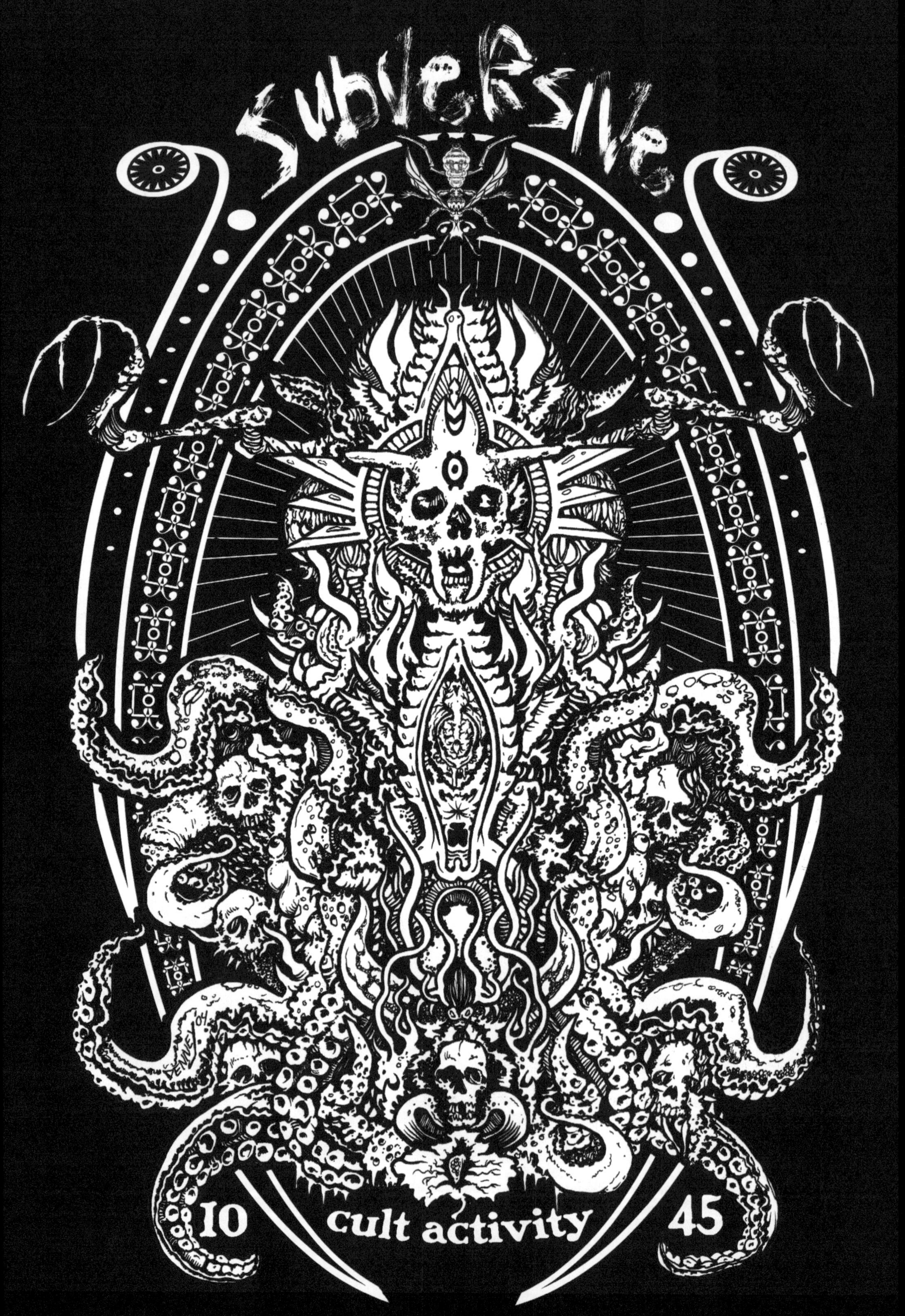
Subversive
10
cult activity
45

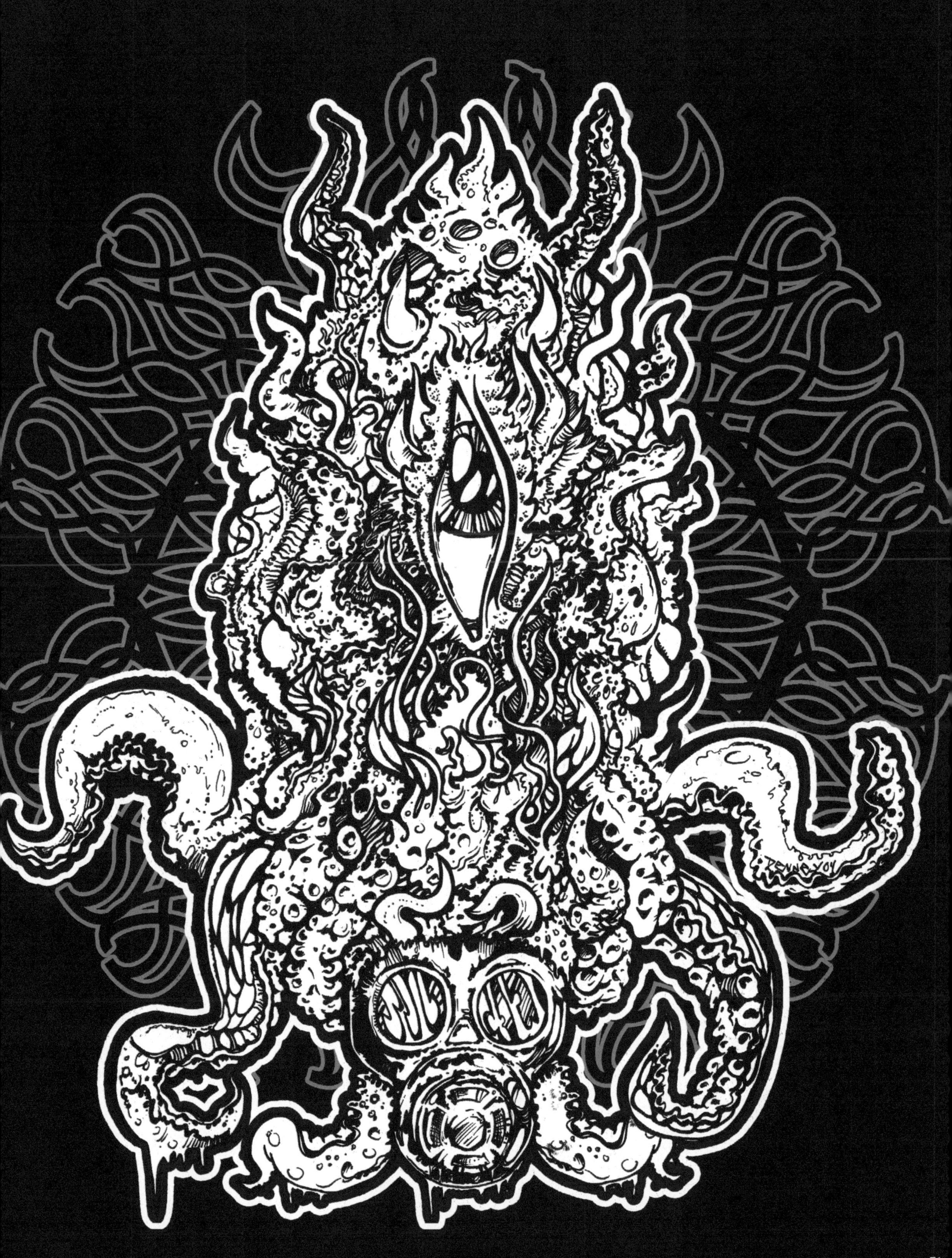

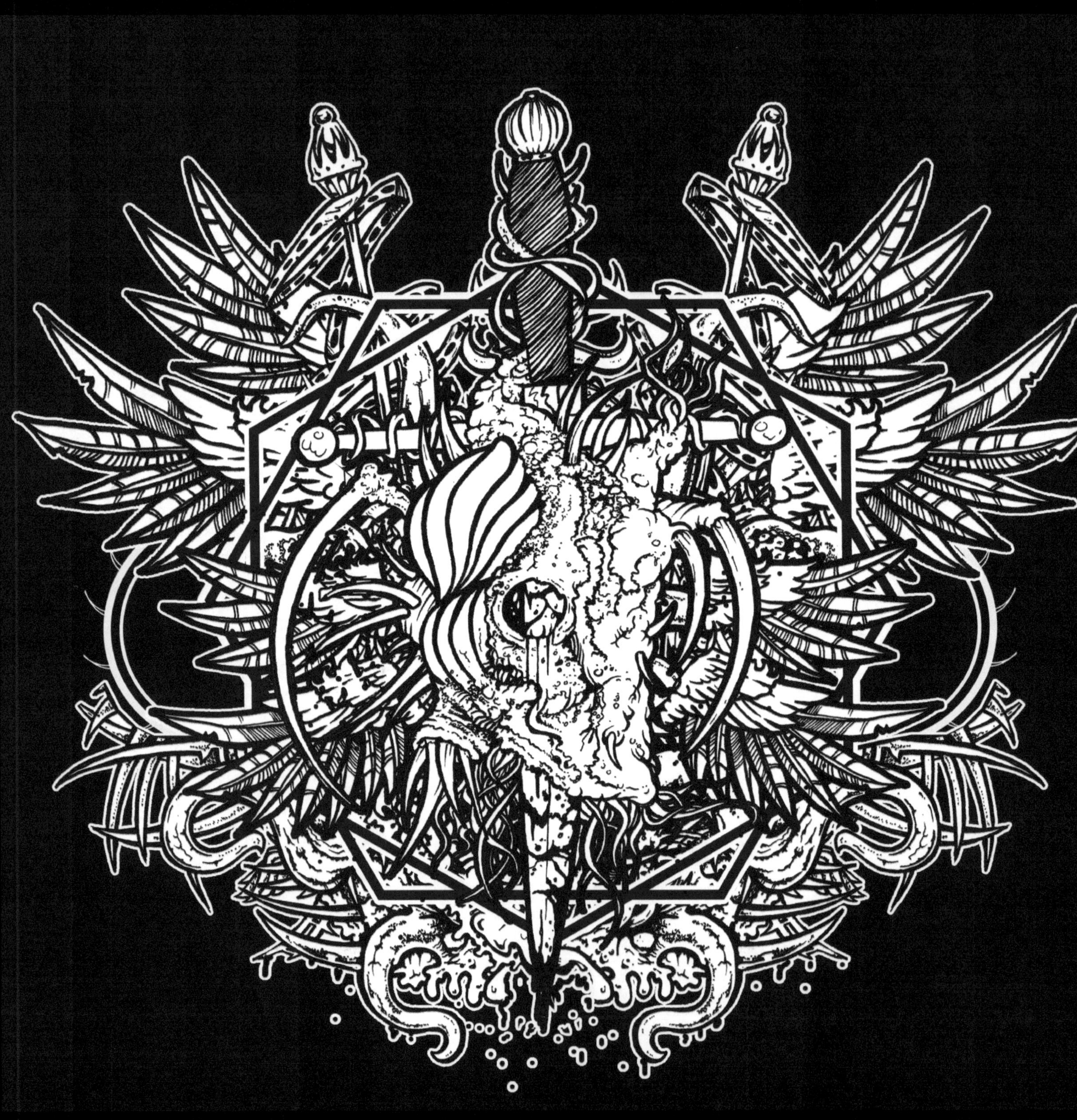

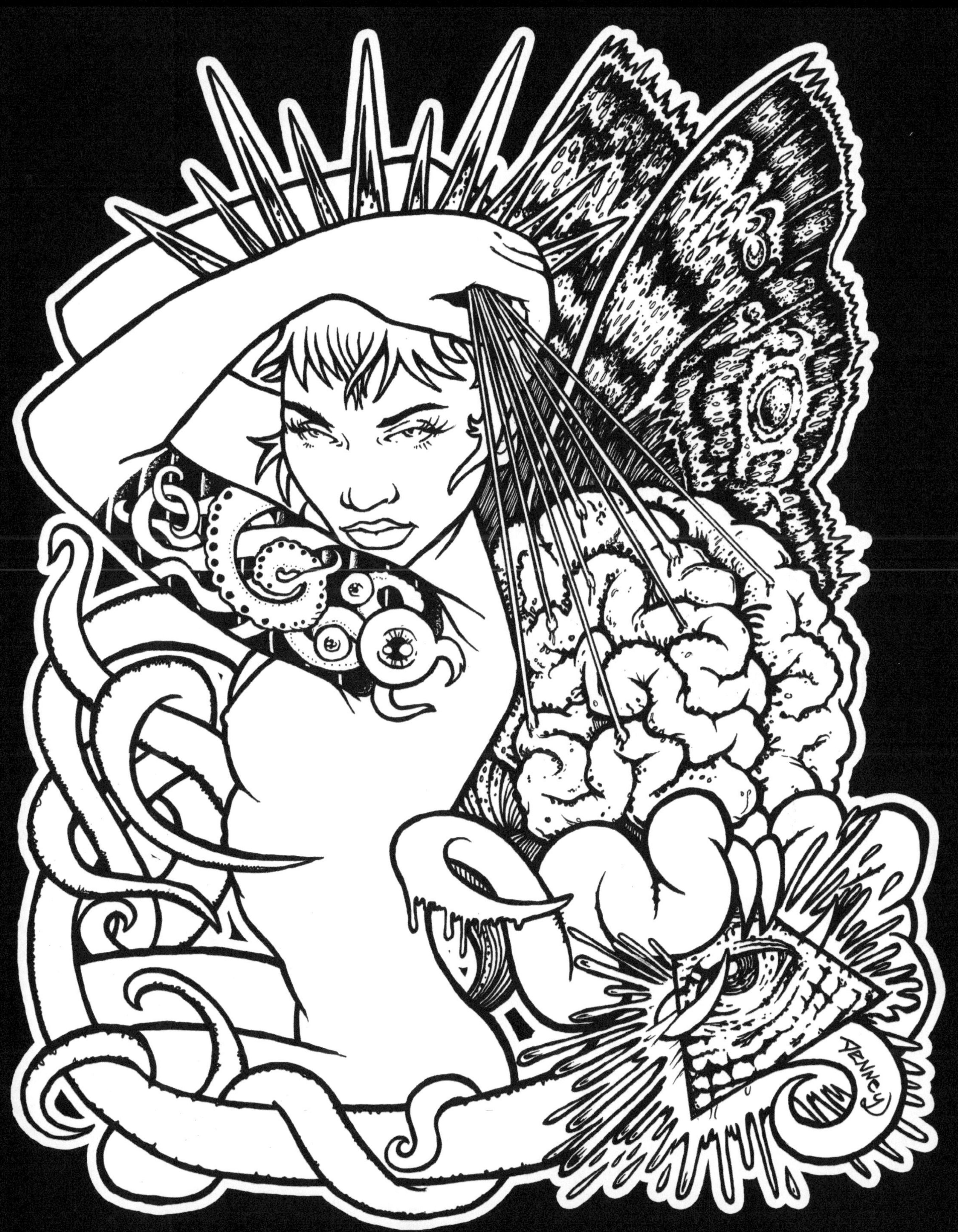

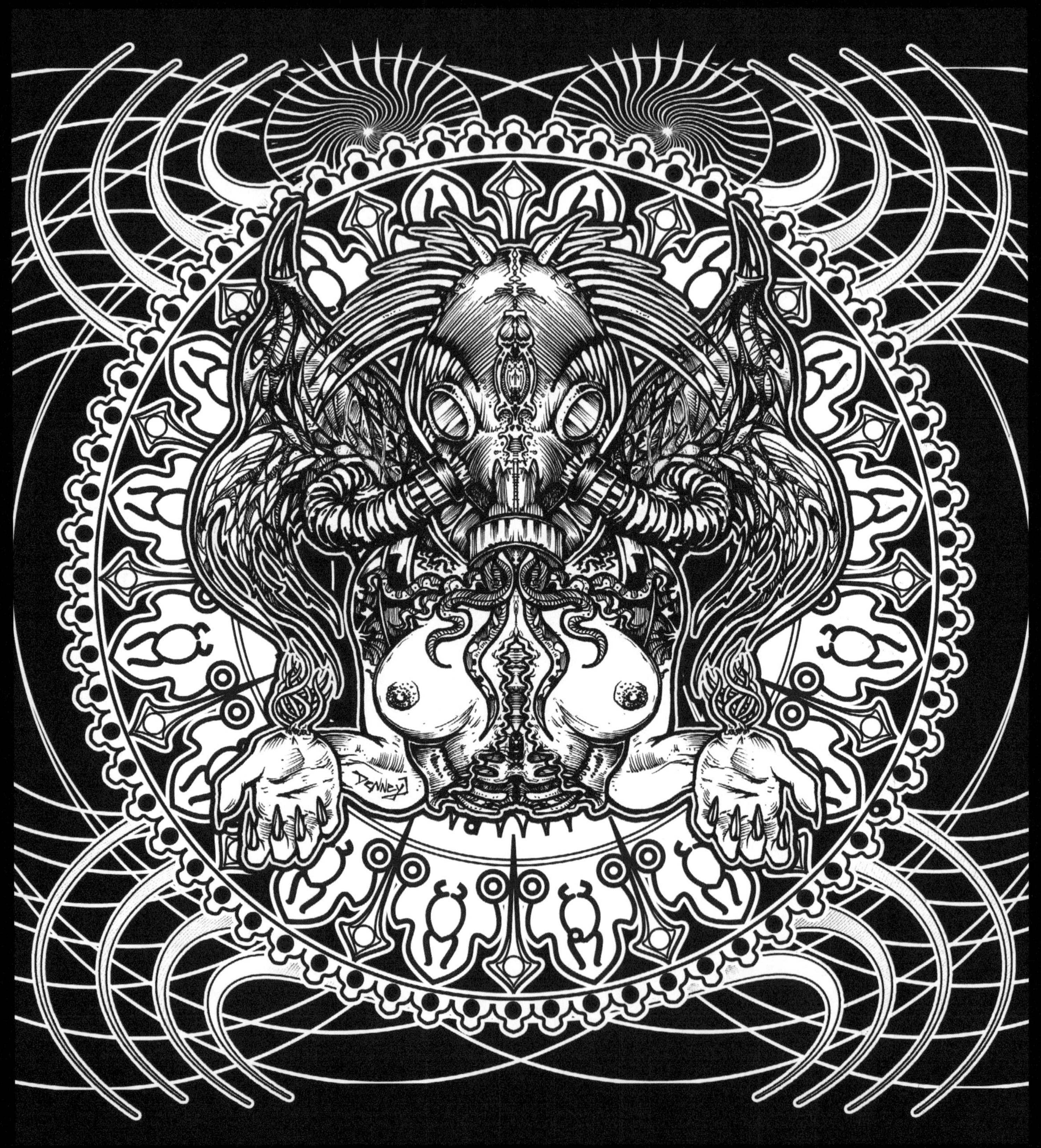
Denney

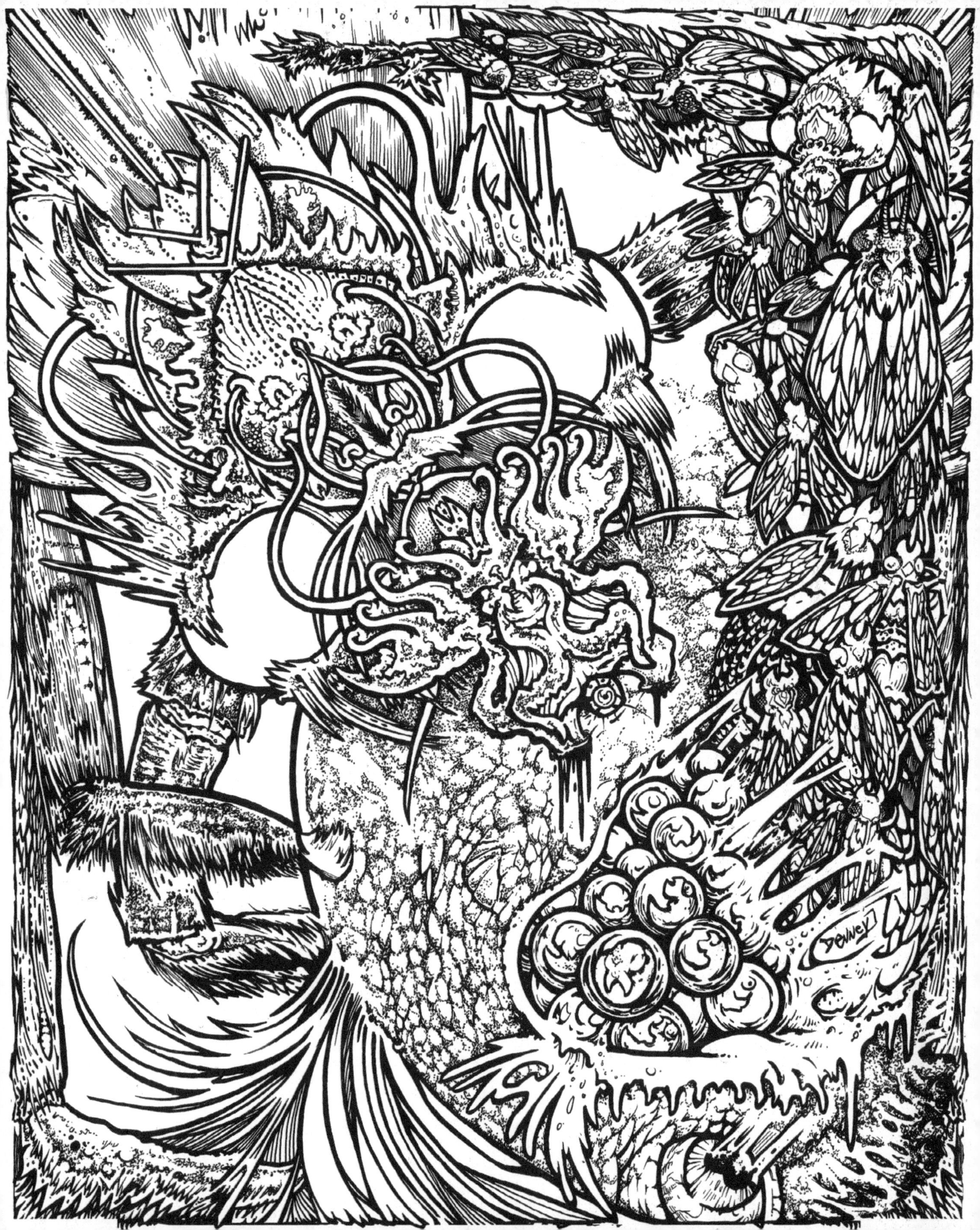
DENNEY

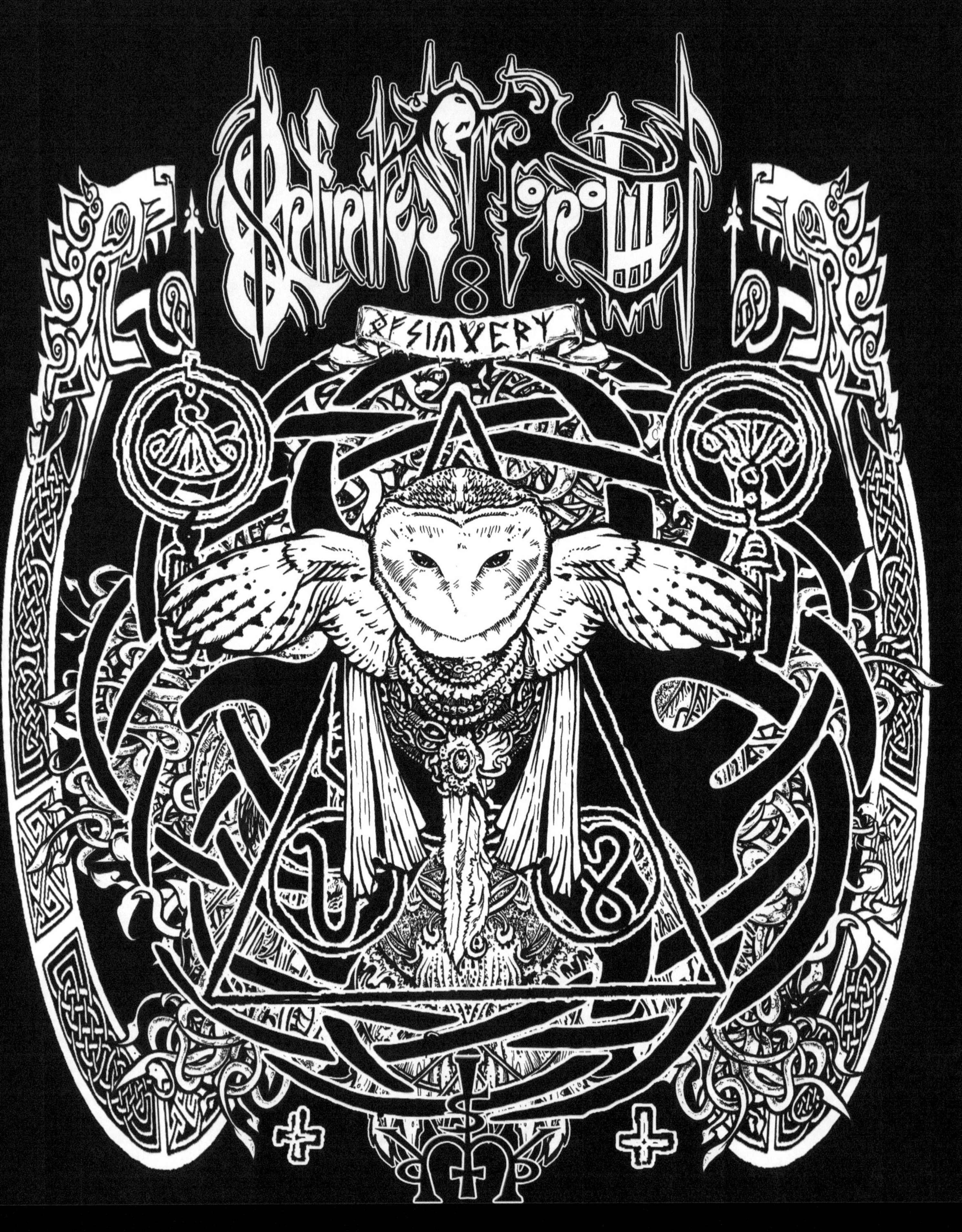

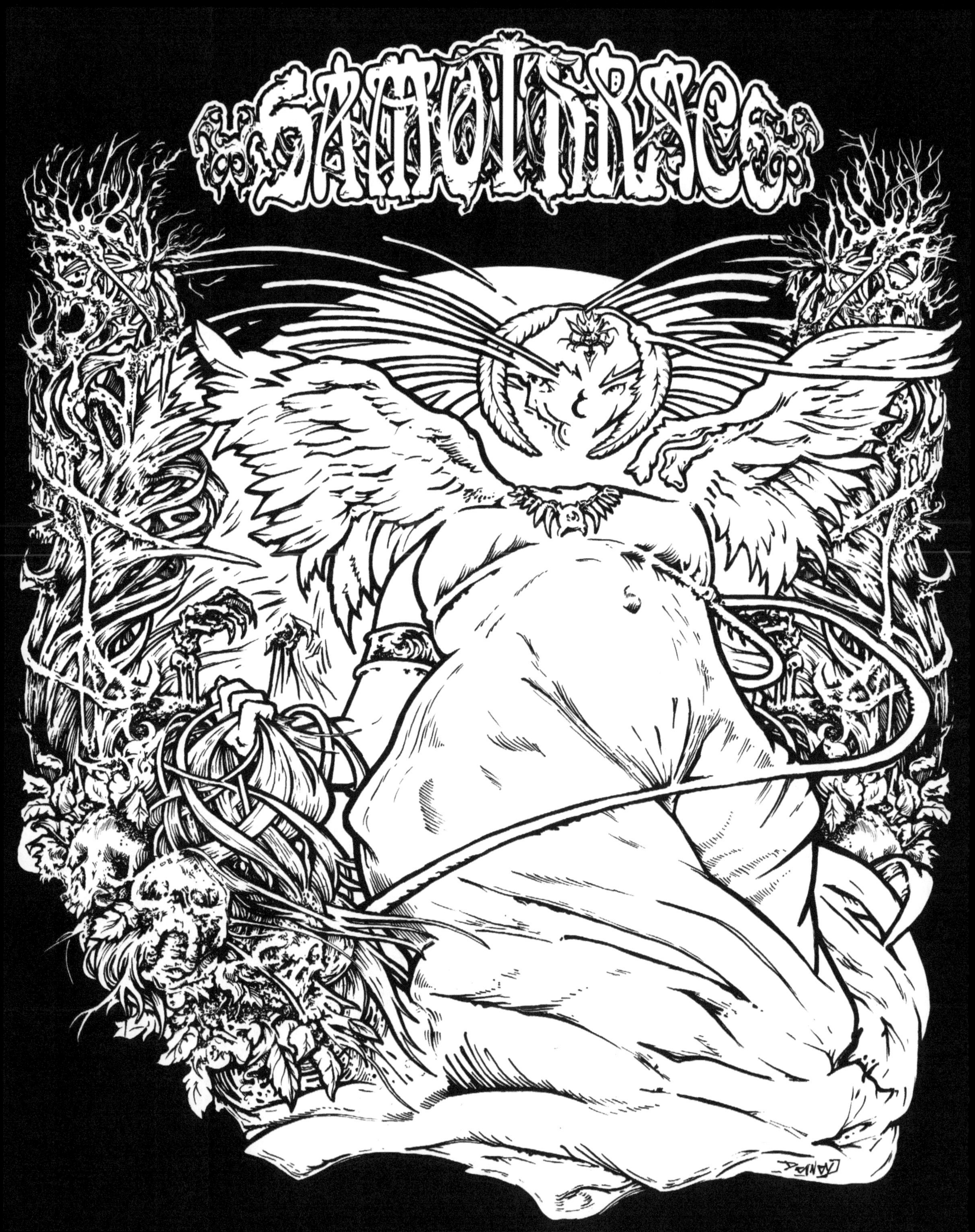
SAMOTHRACE

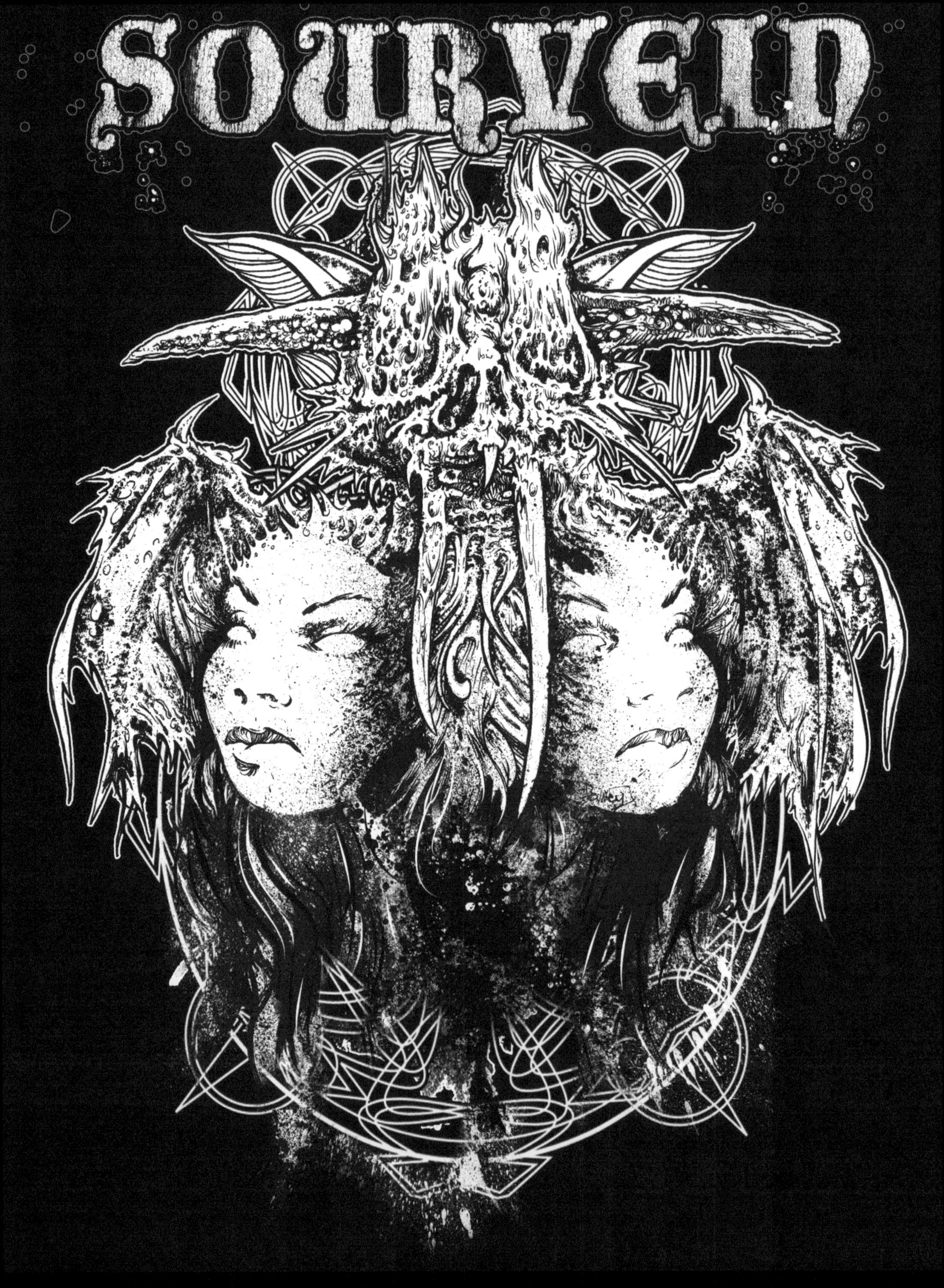

SOURVEIN

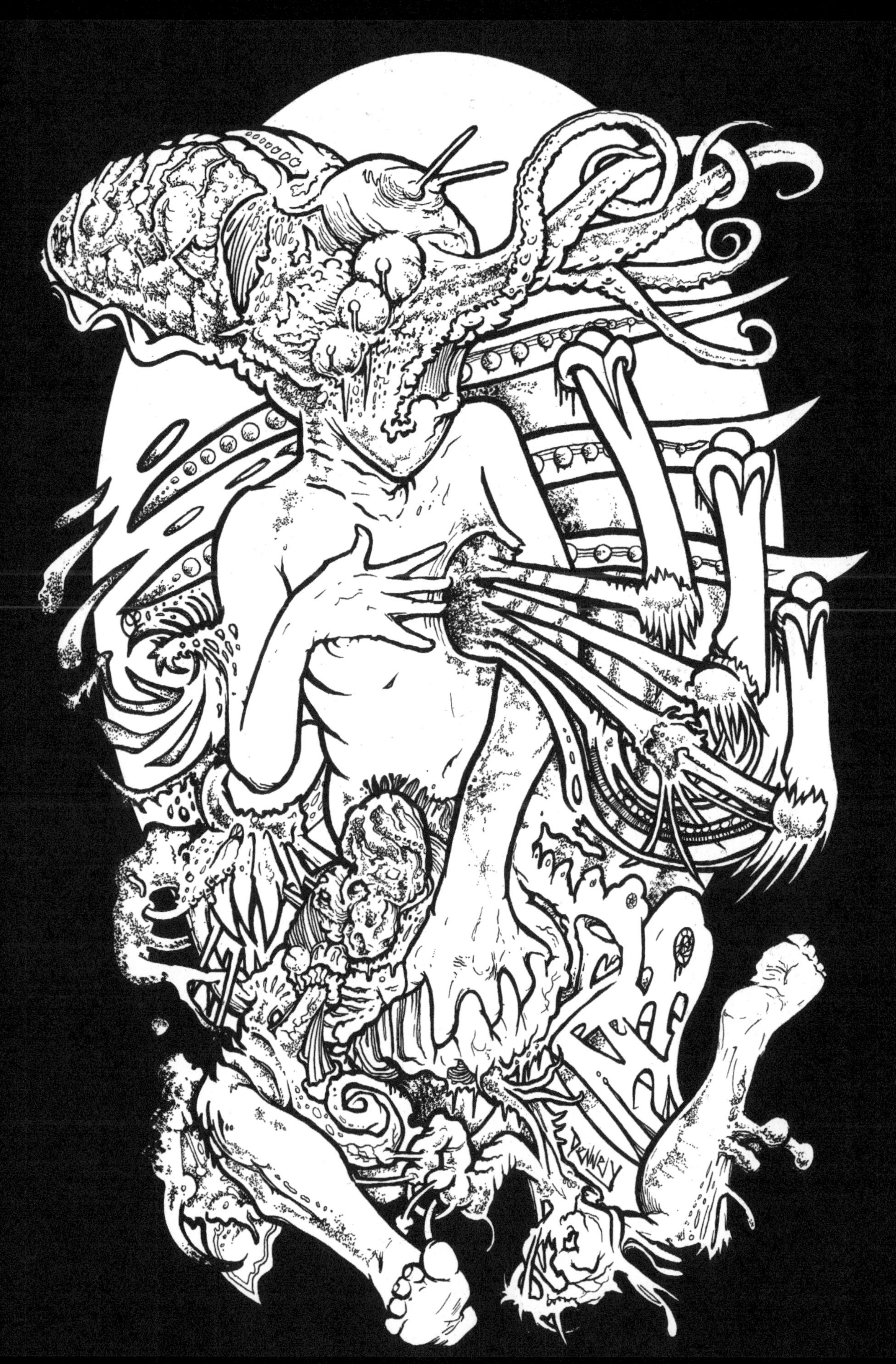

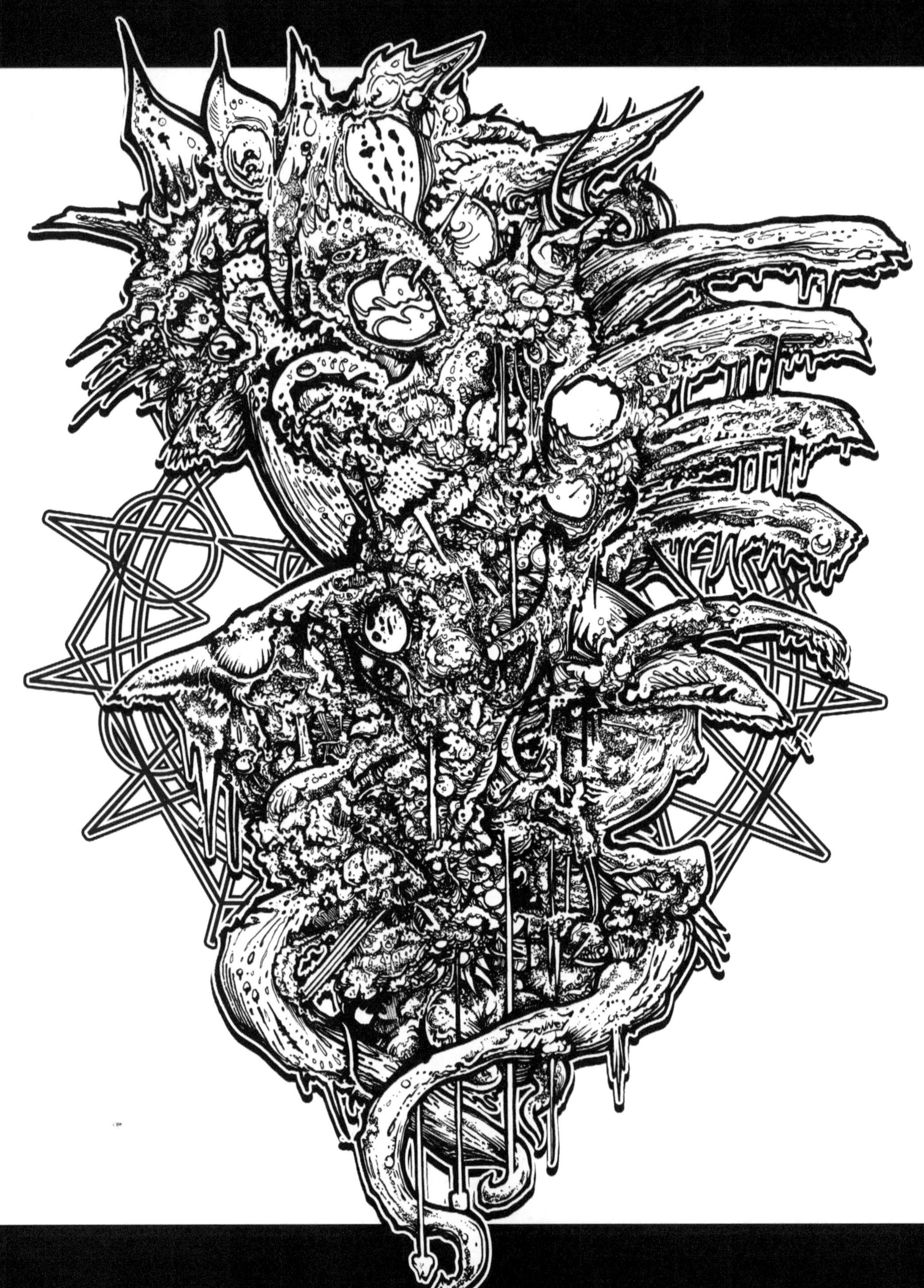

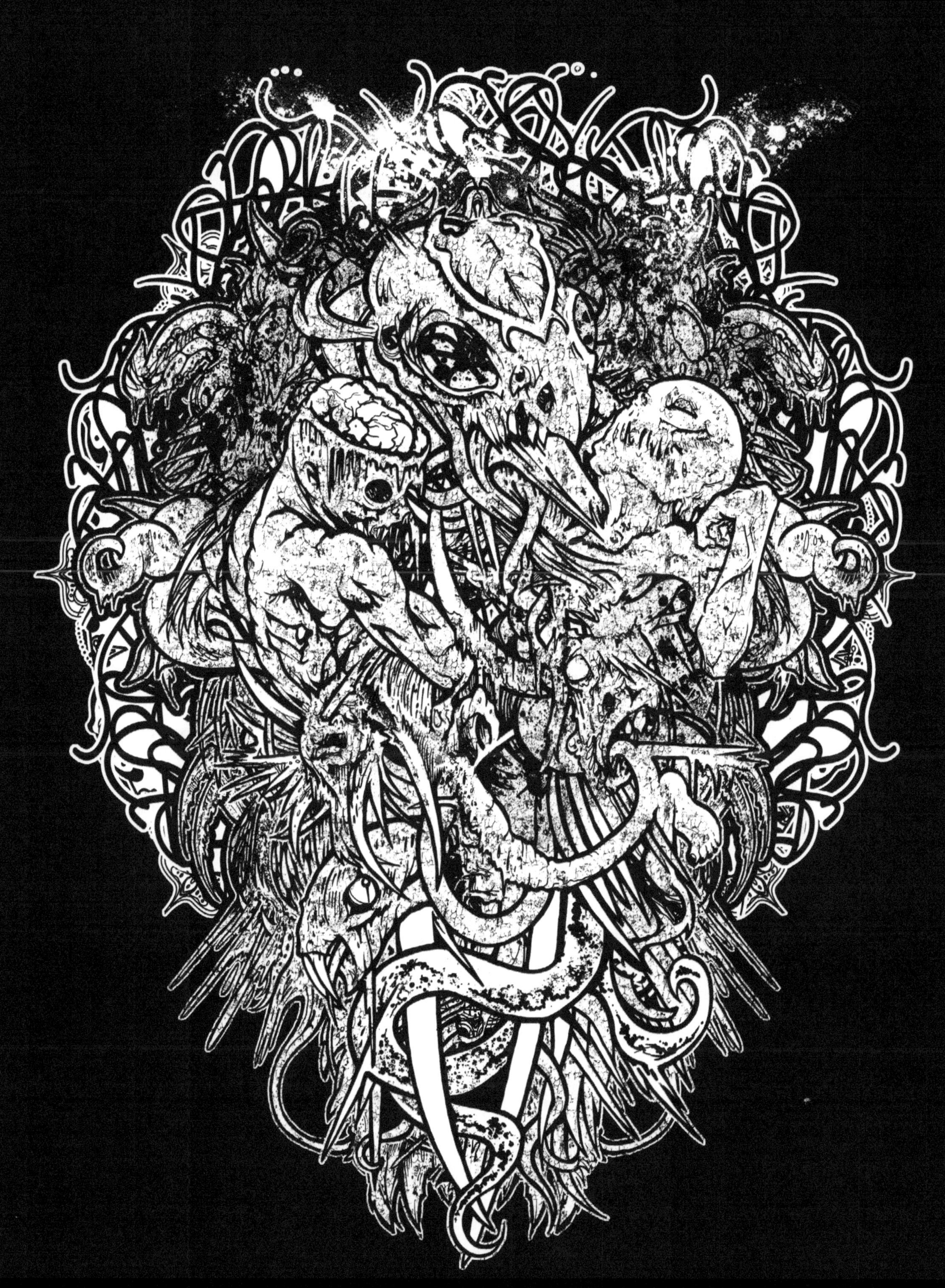

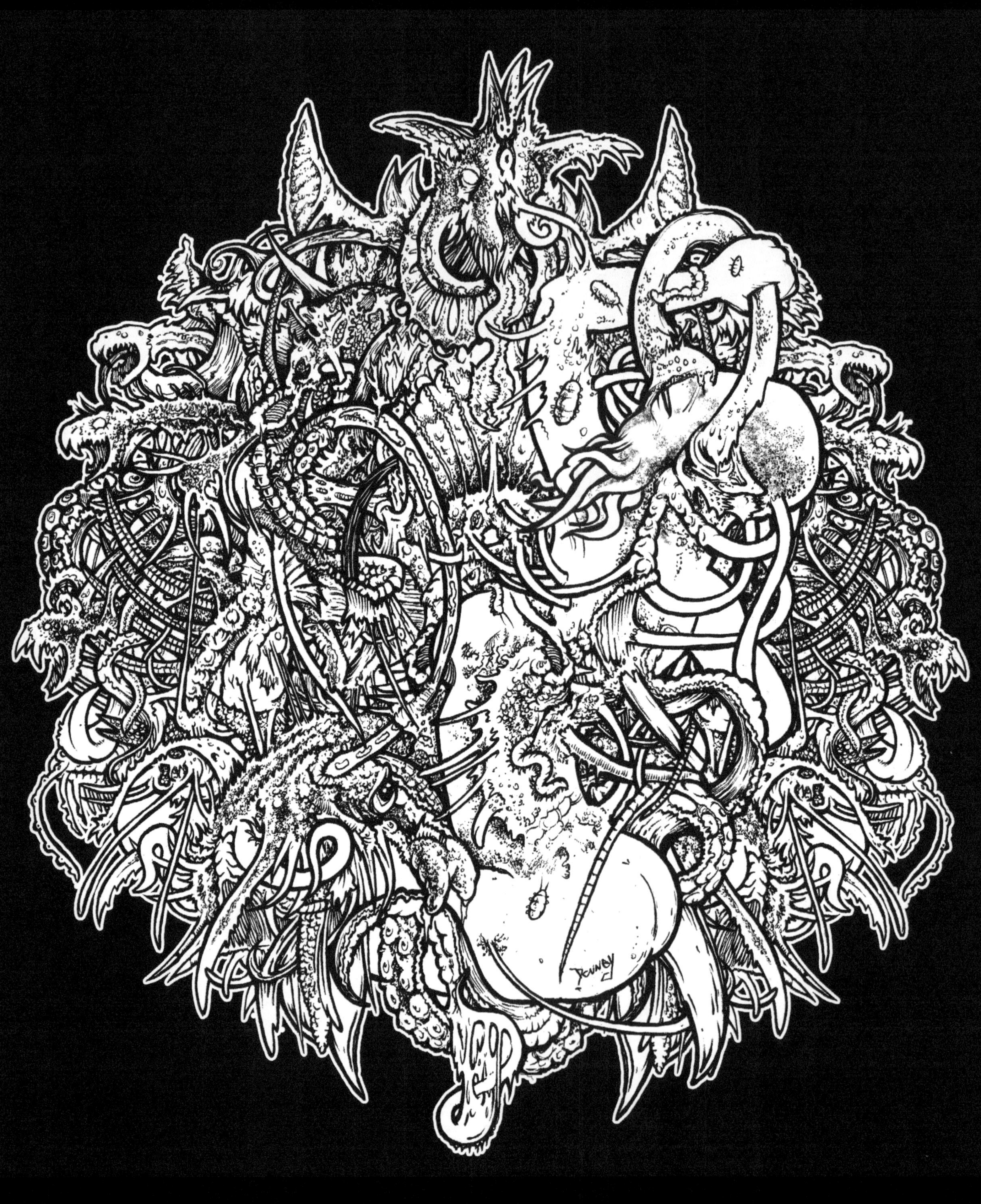

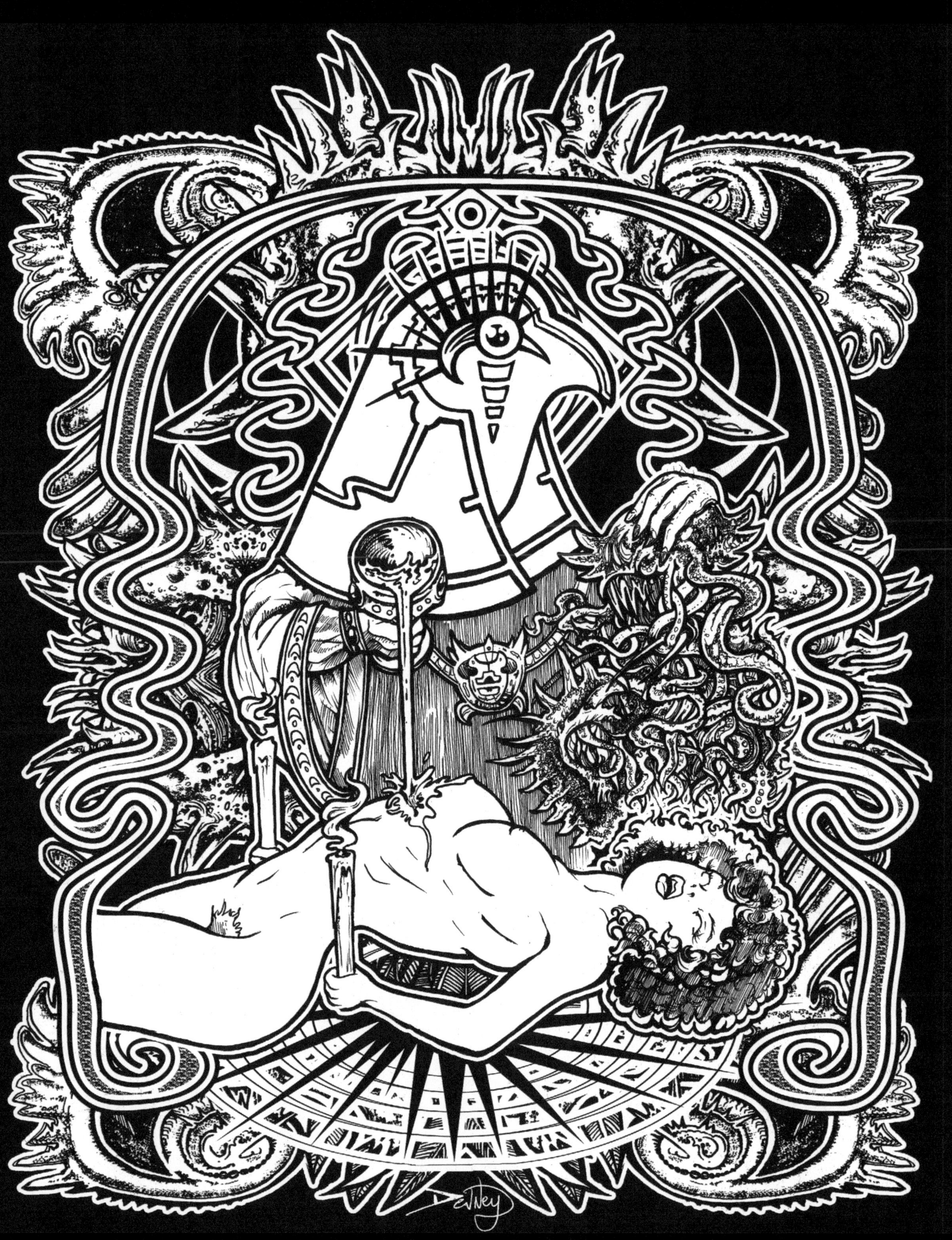
Devney

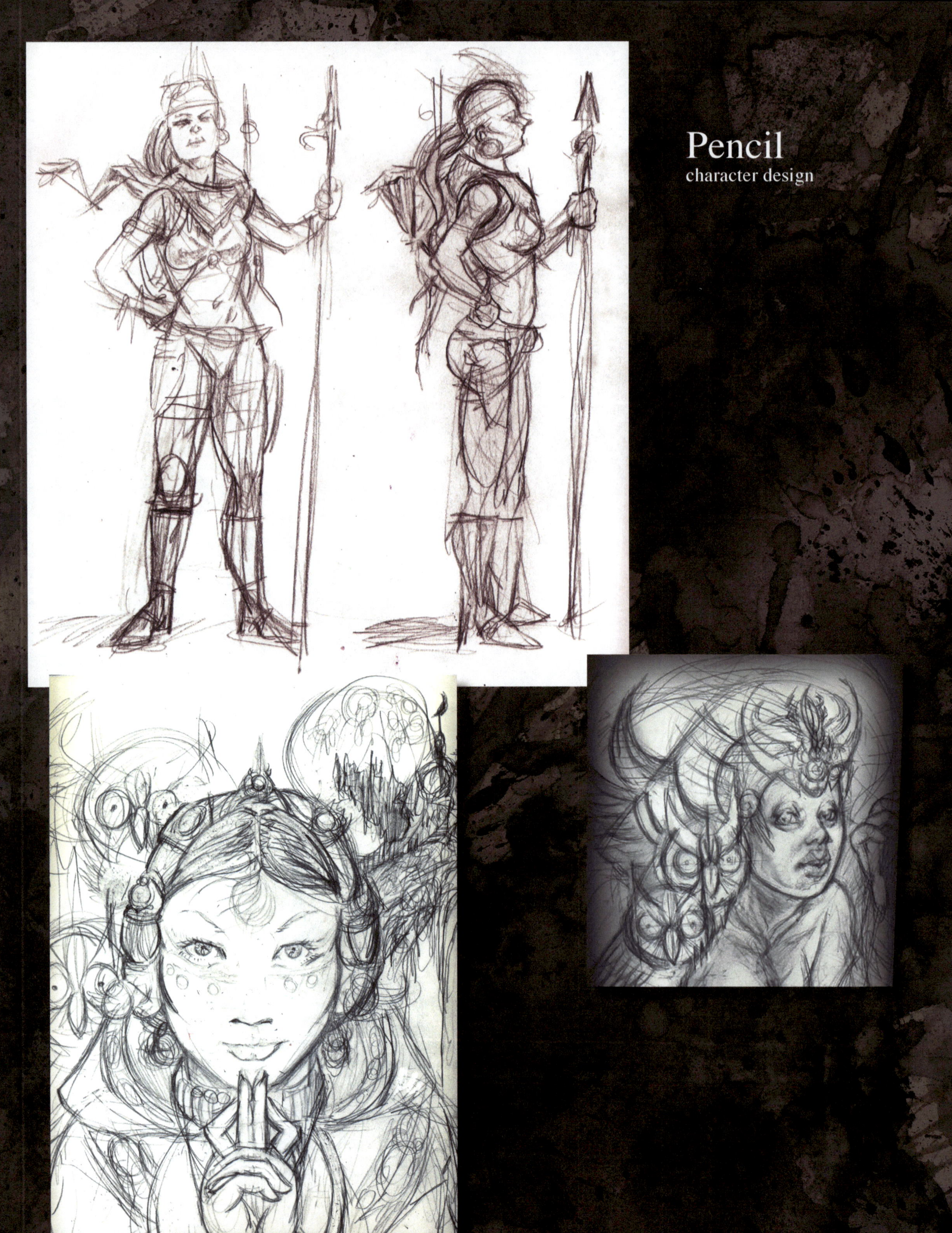

Pencil
character design

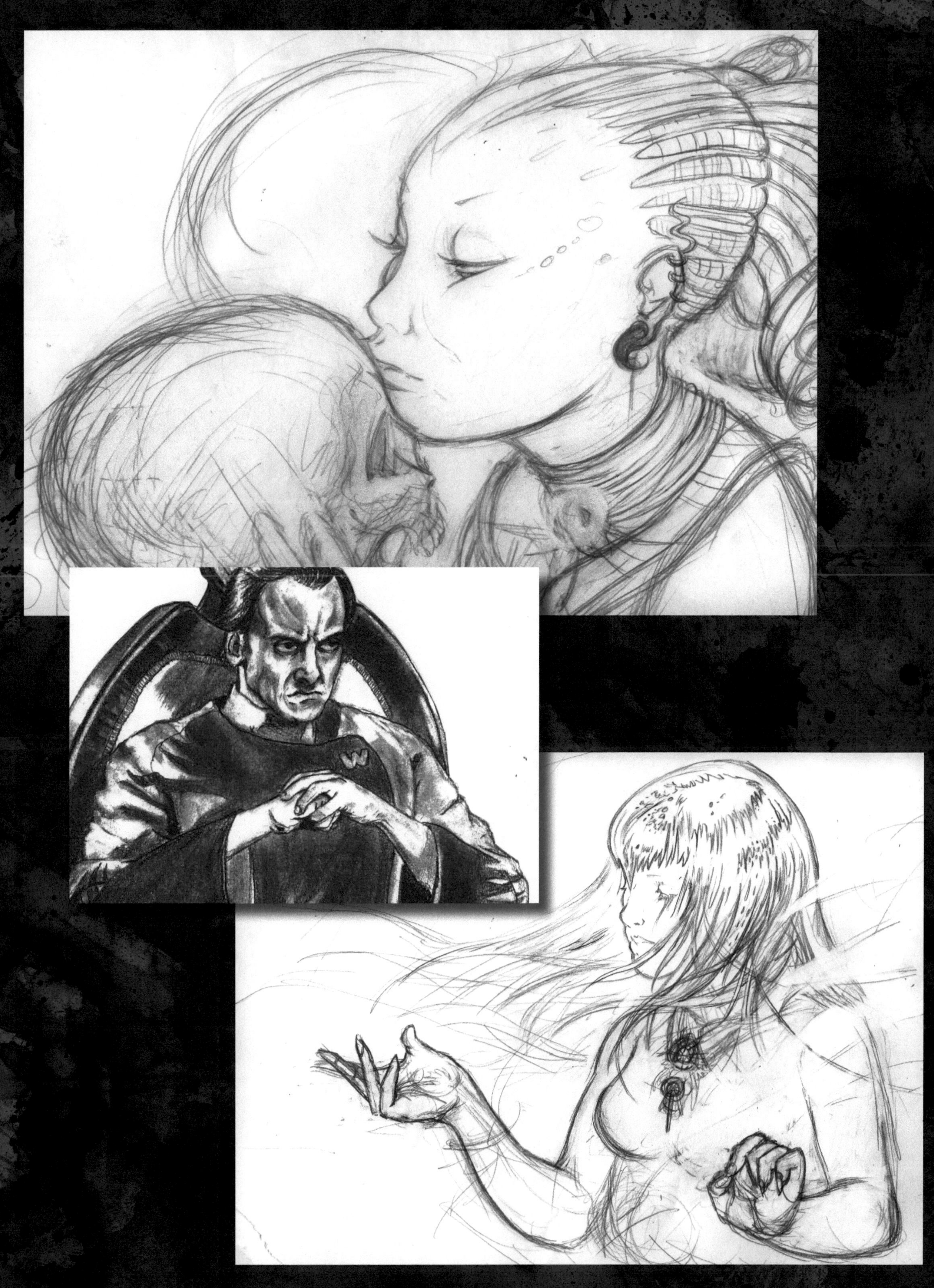

Design

Promo cards and T-Shirts

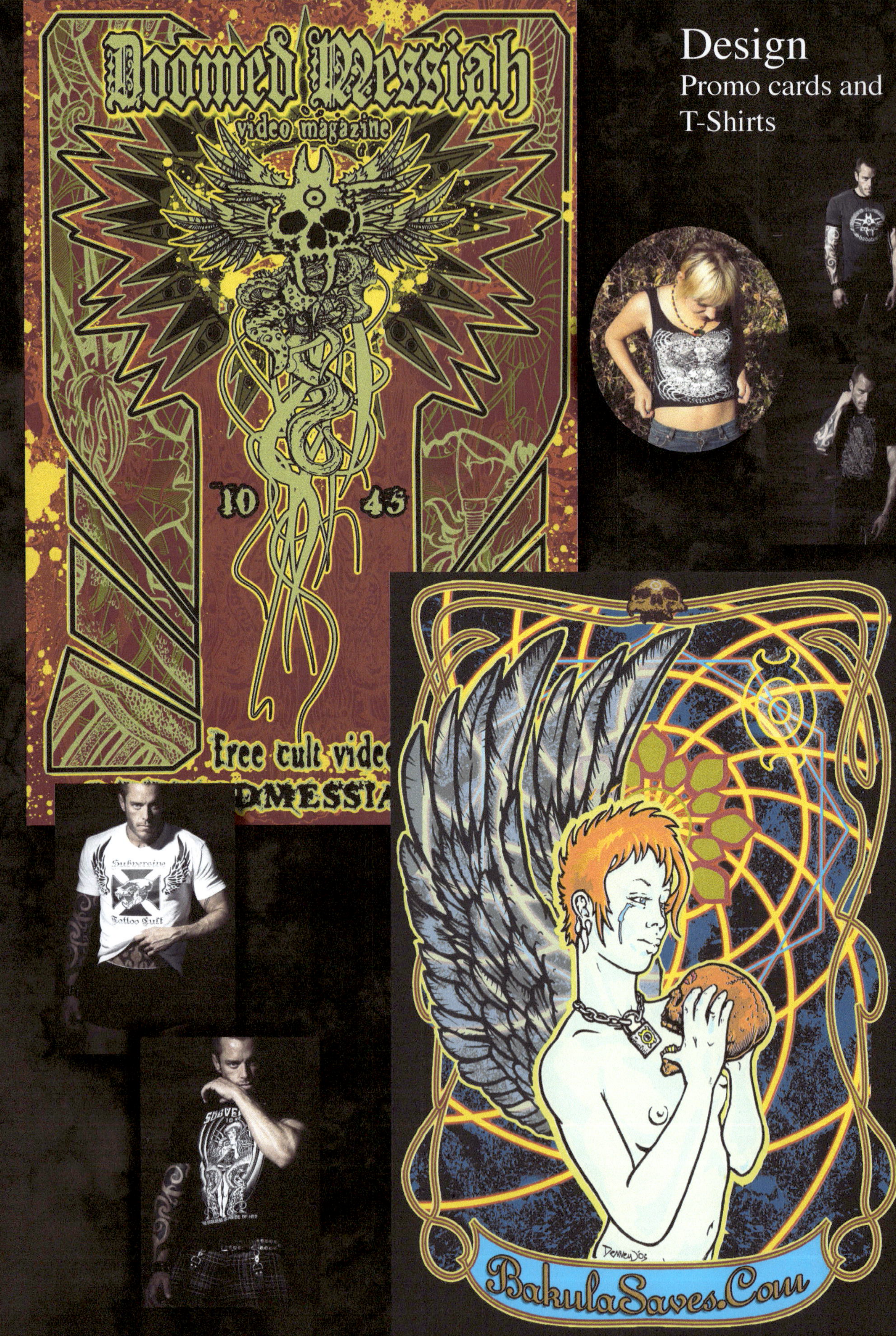

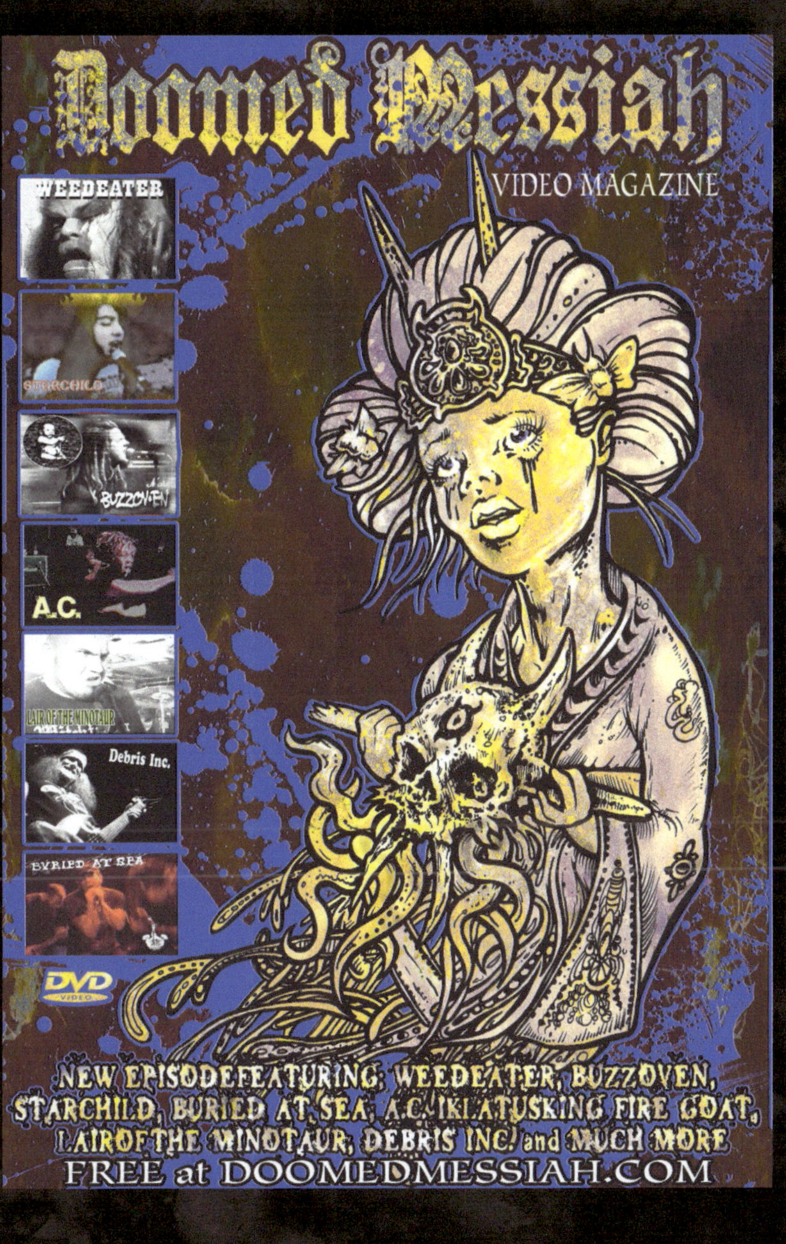
Doomed Messiah
VIDEO MAGAZINE
WEEDEATER
STARCHILD
BUZZOVEN
A.C.
Debris Inc.
BURIED AT SEA
DVD
VIDEO
NEW EPISODEFEATURING: WEEDEATER, BUZZOVEN,
STARCHILD, BURIED AT SEA, A.C., IKLATUSKING FIRE GOAT,
LAIROFTHE MINOTAUR, DEBRIS INC. and MUCH MORE
FREE at DOOMEDMESSIAH.COM

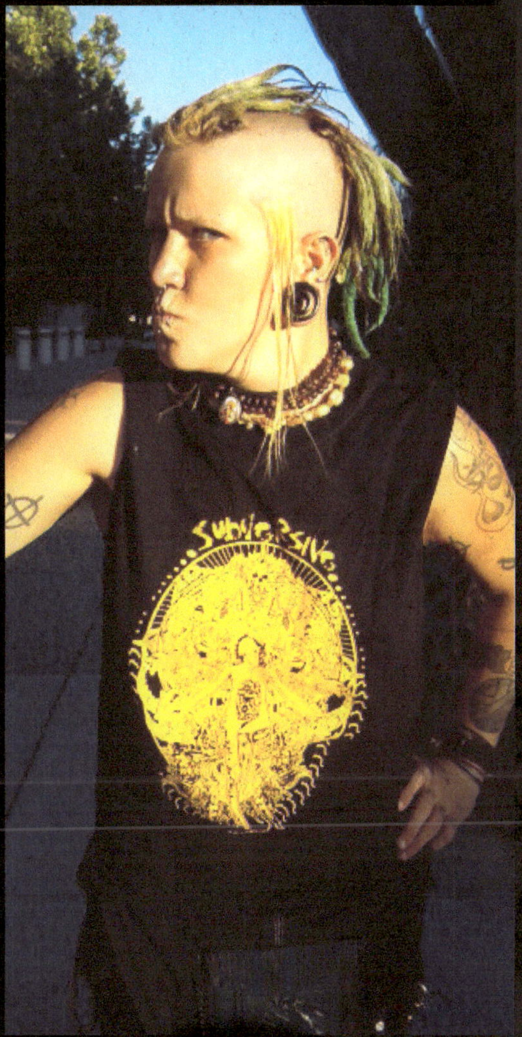

TOM DENNEY
ILLUSTRATION
STORY BOARD
MOTION GRAPHICS
818-450-6558
cyphlon@yahoo.com
BAKULASAVES.COM
myspace.com/bakulasaves

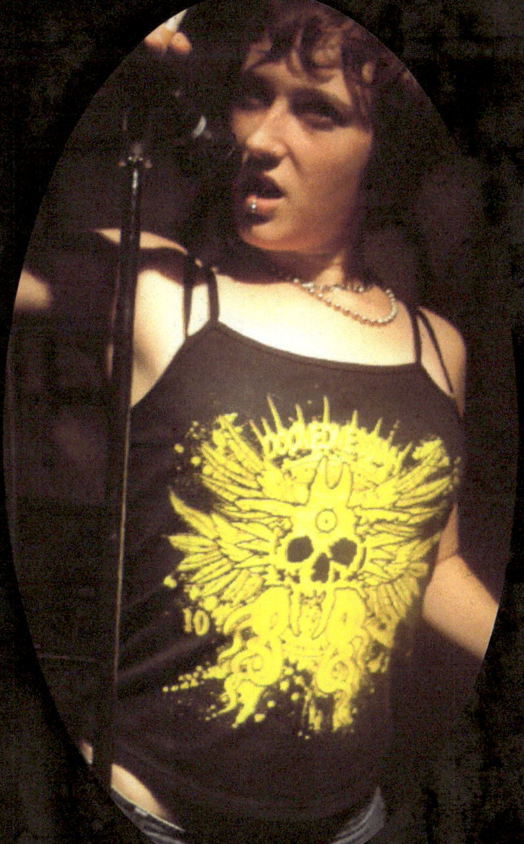

INDEX

Sailing along as a freelance artist since 2002, I have had the opportunity to work with some colorful clients on allot of interesting projects. Here is what a few of them have to say about it.

"Tom is very passionate about music and art. He has a unique vision and an enthusiastic attitude. I always look forward to seeing what he has cooked up in his trippy mind. From the moment I met him several years ago, I knew that I wanted to work with him!"
**-Laura Pleasants,
Kylesa**

"I always thought Tom was on drugs. Then he told me he didn't do drugs. Anyways, I think his art is exceptional and will go down in the annals of rock n roll history. His style helped exemplify our style, which is an appreciation of the old, with a fresh, new approach."
**-Steve Rathbone,
Lair of the Minotuar**

"Tom's twisted, psycho-delic art has been an inspiring force for us"
**-Bruce Lamont,
Yakuza**

"With all of the sick and twisted things Tom Denney puts on paper, I couldnt even begin to imagine what kind of images he has in his own mind. He's helped put an image and presence behind our band."
**-Jonny Davy,
Job For a Cowboy**

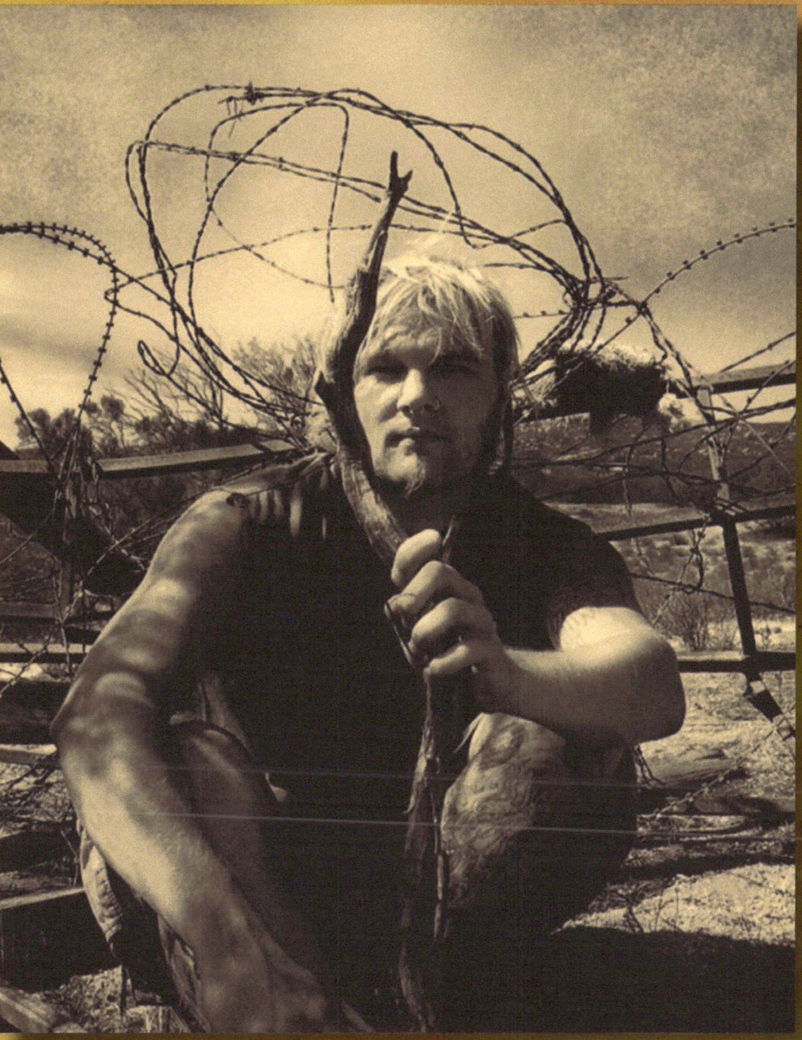

2007- age; 28

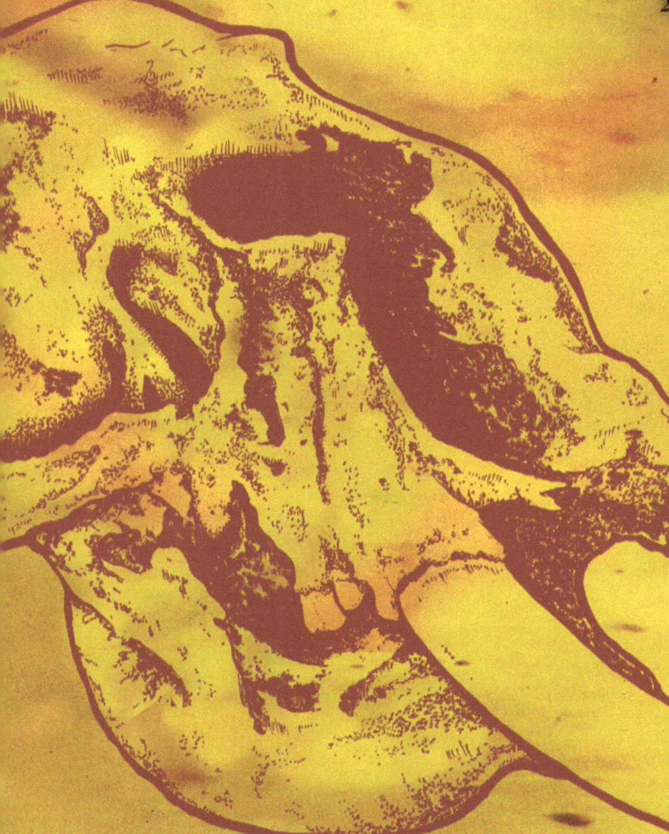

"Tom Denneys' bursting enthusiasm appropriately matches his intense, killer artwork. His heart is in precisely the right place and he has been nothing but a pleasure to work with. Im stoked anytime one of our bands tells us Tom is involved with their artwork."
**-Greg Anderson,
Southern Lord Records**

Pure devastation!!!....... A snap shot into the world of Bakula "I believe" may the rest of the world weep into the soul of Tom Denney to purge forth a new being of enlightenment. Let the scriptures be rewritten, to set ablaze all what we know as the truth. Have the powers to change the minds of slaughtered lambs rotting in the battle fields of I Klatus. We of the born only live to carve history in our own reality, the forces that be blows into this collective sub-straight. Only invested to the grand plan, bring us into the world of vibrations that hum to different frequencies. I have seen the madness that comes into play, waiting for the moment of a doomed messiah to tell us that we are free to just to be.

a simple slave
-Tony Koehl, Artist

"Tom is the best of the best and has a very unique style of artwork that is immediately recognizable. We only have one piece of art from him so far, but we are looking forward to many more. Very professional and timely."
**-Steve Goldberg,
Cephalic Carnage**

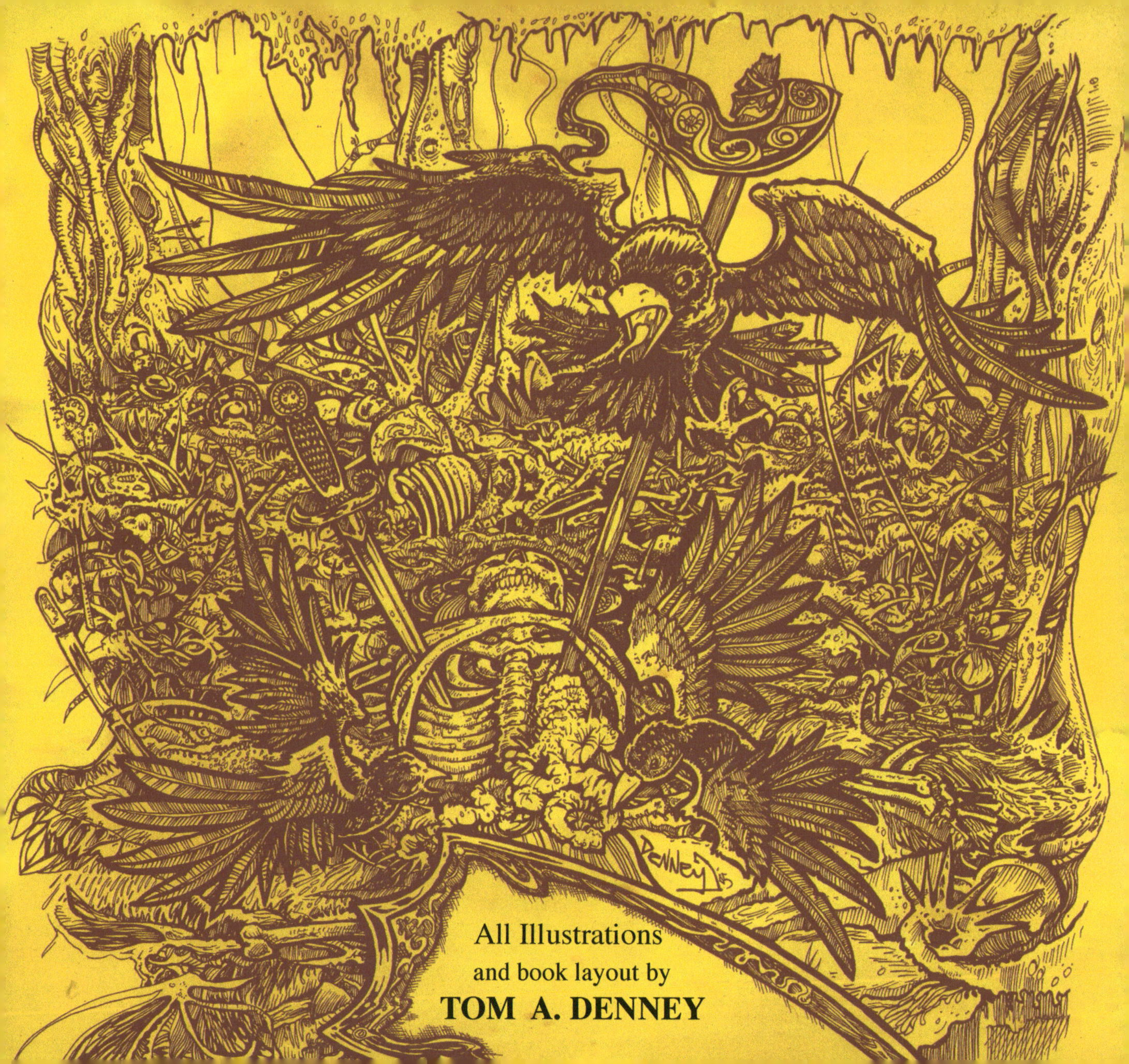

All Illustrations
and book layout by
TOM A. DENNEY

www.ingramcontent.com/pod-product-compliance
Lightning Source LLC
LaVergne TN
LVHW070135110826
845147LV00002B/260

* 9 7 8 0 6 1 5 2 1 9 5 7 8 *